MW01152661

TESTIMONIALS

99

"EVERYONE WANTS TO GROW, BUT TO DATE, THERE HASN'T BEEN A PLAYBOOK ON HOW TO GROW. BROOKE HAS CHANGED THAT WITH THE INDUSTRY'S FIRST PLAYBOOK AND PLATFORM THAT LAYS IT OUT FOR YOU PERFECTLY!"

— Lino Maldonado, Former VP of Operations, Growth & Innovation Wyndham Vacation Rentals

TESTIMONIALS

"The timing of this book couldn't be better. Brooke tackles the hottest topic in the industry with ease, and his expertise is clear from the start."
– Teryn Chapin with Stay Local Nashville

"Brooke is the godfather of growing your inventory. He created the category, and now he's literally written the book on it."
– Matt Tesdall with Family Time Vacation Rentals

"Brooke distills the essence that drove his company from 0 to 500 properties into a system that will work for any VR manager, big or small. He's cracked the code and spelled it out for anyone to create their own growth plan."
– Jed Stevens with Koloa Kai Vacation Rentals

"The best way to grow your inventory is to hire Brooke's company Vintory. The second best way is to read this book."
– Matt Durrette with Cozi Vacation Rentals

"Owner acquisition was a thing, not a science, until Brooke became the Einstein of the category. It's a blueprint for growth."
– Travis Wilburn with Stay Charlottesville

"This is the definitive book on growing your inventory. It could take you years to learn this on your own. But somehow, Brooke has managed to boil it down to something you can consume in a few nights. A must read."
– Paul Becker with Bluewater Vacation Homes

"I absolutely loved this book -- one of the best I've read in a long time! It's entertaining, fast-paced, and inspirational. It's one-part memoir, one-part practical handbook. Brooke lays out exactly what it takes to grow your inventory through specific business lessons with concrete, actionable steps... and zero fluff! No VRM should be without it."
– Cheryl Lantz CEO with Vacation Rental Authority

ACKNOWLEDGEMENTS

I wish to personally thank the following individuals who, without their contribution and support, this book would not have been written:

My Family

My incredibly supportive wife Suzanne and my beautiful, funny, and wicked smart children Mason & Riley. My parents for their unconditional love and support and giving me the winning ovarian lottery ticket of being born in the United States in this generation

My business partners Brian Riggs and Randy Bonds

David Angotti, Wes Melton, and CJ Stam for that fateful breakfast at Merciers that set this entire business into motion

Our "OG" Partners

Our first Partner, CJ Stam, who took a chance on me when I needed it most. Matt Tesdall, John and Kelly Ritch, Steve Surbaugh, Jim and Kelly Willey, Christina and "Thor" Thoreson, Ken and Debbie Furlong

My VRMen brothers and my EO Forum

Vintory Teammates

Unfortunately, I can't possibly list everyone on the team, but without this team, this book would have never been written. I can't say enough about the group we've assembled. Pound for pound, we have built the best team on the planet.

> "
> MY HEART IS WITH THE
> EVERYDAY VACATION RENTAL
> MANAGER WHO SHOWS UP
> EACH DAY WITH A DESIRE TO
> GROW THEMSELVES AND THEIR
> BUSINESS.
> "

TABLE OF CONTENTS

INTRODUCTION

Introduction

My motivation for this book comes from my expertise in growing vacation rental inventory. This is the greatest challenge almost every vacation rental manager faces today.

Since 2007, I have experienced life as a start up in this industry and enjoyed seasons of tremendous growth. I know what it feels like to be the rookie in the room, and I also know what it's like to walk through each phase of growth – from 0 to 500 properties in my portfolio.

Every day, I interact with vacation rental managers across the country. Some are new startups and just want to get their foot in the door. Others are established business owners, but feel like their growth has ground to a halt. Through one-on-one conversations, and the Mastermind groups I lead, I can coach many toward success. It is truly one of the greatest privileges of my life.

Initially, when I started with my first vacation rental company, my only thought was survival. But now that time has passed and a level of success has been achieved, I am able to translate this passion for personal success into the lives of others.

My heart is with the everyday vacation rental manager who shows up each day with a desire to grow themselves and their business. Because I know how hard the journey can be, I want to share the tips and hacks I have learned so they can compete with some of the giants in this industry.

For many vacation rental managers, the thought of competing with large corporations seems daunting. If this sounds like you, my goal is to help you see how this goal is attainable. I'm not promising overnight success, but I am offering some clear-cut steps you can take to bump your business to the next level.

As you will find out in this book, this all starts with inventory. Without it, you don't have a business. It's like having a grocery store without inventory on the shelves. With it, you too can take your business from a small startup to being one of the leaders in the marketplace.

" ...I AM OFFERING SOME CLEAR-CUT STEPS YOU CAN TAKE TO BUMP YOUR BUSINESS TO THE NEXT LEVEL.

WHY SHOULD I GROW?

CHAPTER ONE

Why Should I Grow?

"IF YOU CAN DREAM IT YOU CAN DO IT."

– Walt Disney

Everyone's reason for entering the vacation rental business is different. There isn't exactly a vacation rental school where you go to major in growing your company from 0 to 500 properties.

Few individuals decide out of college to get in the vacation home rental business. Honestly, it can be a bit of a tough market to jump into if you have no experience or reputation, and acquiring those first couple properties can be a mammoth challenge! And as you may have already discovered, few realtors or business owners want to refer their clients to someone without a proven track record.

Often, people stumble into the vacation rental business through necessity or opportunity. For example, at the height of the 2008 financial crisis, many vacation homeowners suddenly found themselves in a pinch and needed extra cash. Prior to this point, their business might have been doing fine and they saw no issue leaving a property sit vacant for ten months out of the year. But when pressures rose and finances got tight, they were forced into the vacation rental space through necessity.

Such was my story. I started my first company in the mortgage industry at the ripe age of twenty-five.

After several years of working at another job as an employee, I thought to myself, "I can do this better." This self-assurance prompted me to put the wheels of change in gear to say my goodbye. But about this same time, my boss learned of my plans and my departure was accelerated.

Several months prior to my intended farewell, my wife and I got married. It was September 1999 and a couple days later we flew to Hawaii for our honeymoon. It was then I received an unexpected call. I found out my boss realized I was starting my own mortgage company and he made the decision to fire me on the spot – along with several others in my department. Hanging up the phone, I made my way back down to the pool where my wife was sipping a Lava Flow (a delicious frozen drink made up of strawberry daiquiri and pina colada which I highly recommend!) and I pronounced to her, "Well, honey, you just married an unemployed man!"

Days after our honeymoon ended, we returned home to Baltimore, and I founded First Commonwealth Funding. And for the next eight years my company skyrocketed. We grew to over a hundred employees, were licensed in twelve states, and were closing over $350 million in loans a year. It was an incredible ride and I felt on top of the world. I had all the toys, vacations, and prestige one could want at my age.

But then came the financial crisis and everything changed. Because the mortgage business was the first to feel this impact, my company's crash began in 2007. Over the course of a year, I watched the company I built from the ground up crumble before my eyes. We went from closing around thirty million a month in loans to about a tenth of that in the span of months. On top of this, because we had grown so fast, we found ourselves with a ton of overhead, including our twenty thousand square foot class A facility.

While I felt terrible and partially responsible for our team's collapse, everyone around me could take one look at the mortgage industry and see the writing was on the wall. Company after company folded and it was only a matter of time before we did the same.

To make matters worse, much of my parents' retirement was tied up in the success of the business and so the failure I experienced affected not only my team, but those who raised me. I had two small children and my wife was a stay-at-home mom. So many people were depending on me, and I could not escape the feeling I had let everyone down. Let's just say there were a good number of sleepless nights.

But then, an unexpected lifeline dropped. At the time, I was part of this group called the Young Presidents' Organization (YPO) and one of the other men in the group was this guy named Brad Callahan.

Brad was a very successful entrepreneur who founded and oversaw multiple organizations. Seeing the collapse of the mortgage industry, he invited me to lunch at Legal Sea Foods in Baltimore and said, "Brooke, I've had the idea to start a vacation rental company for over five years and think you're the guy I would like to run it."

My initial thought was, "Vacation rentals? Doesn't this

guy know that we are in the midst of a recession?" But the more I thought about it, the more the idea grew on me. We spent the next two hours writing out the business plan on the back of our menu and that was the launching point of what became Vantage Resort Realty.

At some point, I remember speaking with one of my attorneys on the phone and sharing my reluctance to let go of my business and step out into the unknown of this new venture. His response took me by surprise. "Brooke, hang up right now and tell Brad you are going to take the job!" He went on to explain that so many people who were in the mortgage business didn't have a parachute like this to get them out and that I should stop overthinking the situation. That brief conversation gave me added perspective and was just the nudge I needed.

Looking back, I can understand my reluctance to say goodbye to my mortgage business. As an entrepreneur, I am an eternal optimist by nature. When others around me say it can't be done, I put my head down and get back to work figuring out a new solution.

So, on one side, I felt awful and thought there must be some way I can make this work. But inside I knew I was making the right decision and I was excited about starting something fresh. I loved the challenge of learning something new and then putting this knowledge into action.

STARTING FROM SCRATCH... AGAIN

"ADVERSITY CAUSES SOME MEN TO BREAK AND OTHERS TO BREAK RECORDS."

— William Arthur Ward

While few parts of this transition were easy, I was able to take away many of the lessons in the mortgage business and use them in the vacation rental industry.

One of the lessons the vacation rental business taught me was that I could not import my street credibility as a mortgage banker and expect new clients to give me any level of respect. From the start, I began making the three-hour commute every Monday from Baltimore to Ocean City, only to return on the weekend and start the same process over again the next week.

By my geographical location, I was an outsider. In those early months, I would pitch the vision of the company to local residents and their response was often predictable. "Do you know how many people have come across the Bay Bridge and have failed?"

I could see their point. Here I was, pitching an upstart business in a field I knew little about. And each time I crossed the four plus miles of the Chesapeake Bay, I struggled with all sorts of imposter syndrome feelings.

At the start, Vantage Resort Realty was anything but a household name in the broader Ocean City community. We were shunned and laughed at by those who were already in this space.

But all of this was about to change. As I studied the competition in the Ocean City area, I realized how many vacation rental managers (VRMs) were not even doing the basics. For example, when guests checked into their rental units, they were expected to bring their own sheets, towels, and toilet paper. Let's just say their experience was anything but posh. It was basically, "Here are your keys, here is your room, get the heck out!"

This did not sit well with me, and I knew taking a different approach could be effective. And so instead of treating guests like they were an inconvenience, we focused on providing what I would call a four-star guest experience. We weren't going to be the Bellagio of Vegas, but we could set ourselves apart from the competition by doing the basics with excellence.

And even though our first year was tight and I was forced to take a significant reduction in salary, the hard work began to pay off. I was working fourteen to fifteen hours a day, doing whatever I could to help us succeed. By year two, we began to gain traction and over the course of the next four years, I took a fledgling startup and turned it into a company of over five hundred properties.

KEEP FOCUSED ON WHAT DRIVES YOU

As a Vacation Rental Manager (VRM), your drive to succeed is linked to one of five types of personalities. As you look at each of these personas, ask yourself which one best describes you.

PERSONALITY 1: THE ENTREPRENEUR VRM

The Entrepreneur VRM is motivated by growth. They like to lead and are constantly looking for new opportunities. They prioritize business development, thrive off of the numbers, and want to take their business to the next level. They take pride in helping their homeowners achieve their own growth goals and they are well connected to the network, resources, and talent they need to make their vision a reality.

Entrepreneur VRMs are focused on growth. From the moment they start the business, they have a potential exit strategy in mind. Often, their mindset is to grow their business as large as they can and then cash out. They are focused on revenue management and long for the day they can hand their keys to someone who will prioritize the return on their investment.

PERSONALITY 2: THE COMMUNITY HEART VRM

The Community Heart VRM is a champion of their community and location. They are passionate about bringing others to their destination and helping them unlock local treasures. They are fierce advocates and community supporters, and know that their community is their competitive advantage. They are proud to reinvest back in the community they love.

Their "why" is to invest in and share the community they love. They are knowledgeable and have a heart for their location. They want to feel like their home is in good hands while they are away, and to feel like they are partners with a company that is as passionate about their community as they are.

PERSONALITY 3: THE HOSPITALITY HOST VRM

The Hospitality Host VRM finds joy in serving others. They know it's not enough to deliver great service, and they define their business by the relationships they build with homeowners and the hospitality they provide their guests. They are driven to prove that the vacation rental industry can offer advantages that a hotel cannot match, and they're ready to welcome guests to the ultimate way to travel, rest, and play!

Hospitality Host VRMs seek to provide a partnership homeowners and guests can trust. Their strengths include: building meaningful relationships that attract and retain homeowners and guests, and ensuring others enjoy a home they are proud of. Plus, these VRMs want to experience the perks of full-service management so that when they arrive at their home away from home, it is *guest ready* for them to personally enjoy. They appreciate hospitality and want to know they will be taken care of.

PERSONALITY 4: THE PROBLEM SOLVER VRM

The Problem Solver VRM is driven to provide the best services to their homeowners and guests. They thrive off doing things better than the competition. Whether it's maintenance, guest services, or delivering peace of mind to those who pass them their keys, this VRM takes pride in providing a full-service experience every guest can count on.

Problem Solver VRMs target leads tend to be people who aren't happy with their current property manager, or they're tired of doing it themselves. Either way, they're looking for someone they can trust with their keys. They want to know their home is cared for without the headaches or stress they'll have if property management isn't "done right."

PERSONALITY 5: THE MEMORY MAKER VRM

The Memory Maker VRM values the opportunity to provide the backdrop for shared memories between friends and families. They know how powerful a vacation space can be to make life-long memories and their goal is to give this gift to as many homeowners and guests as possible.

The "why" for Memory Maker VRMs is to give and protect the precious time loved ones spend on vacation. Their strengths are minimizing stress, while maximizing joy, peace of mind, and comfort. They want to enjoy their vacation home whenever they want, and to benefit from the same services and perks their guests receive. They want this partnership to be stress-free, relaxed, and allow them to still enjoy time in their home.

EVERYONE'S WHY IS DIFFERENT

"GREAT COMPANIES DON'T OFFER US SOMETHING TO BUY. GREAT COMPANIES OFFER US SOMETHING TO BUY INTO."

– Simon Sinek

It's likely you might be familiar with Simon Sinek's book or TED Talk *Start with Why* in which he outlines the importance of knowing the reason we do what we do.

While I would like to say there were all these wonderful reasons I had for getting into the vacation rental space, the truth is, I was desperate! I needed to do something to take care of my family and maintain the lifestyle I enjoyed.

As it turns out, my journey is not uncommon.

Take the story of my friend Angie Leone. She and her husband Mike moved to Maui in 2006 for Angie to take up a job as a speech pathologist. In a roundabout manner, they found their way into the vacation rental industry through an unexpected opportunity.

Soon after the birth of her first child, Angie began to rent their condo in West Maui to people on vacation. But this simple step had a ripple effect, and it wasn't long before other friends and neighbors recruited Angie to manage their properties. This evolved into Angie launching her own company, Coconut Condos, and today Angie manages over sixty luxury condos in the West Maui community.

What I love about Angie's passion is that she isn't in this business solely for the money. As she stated on a recent podcast episode, "When it really became our family business, I had to find something that motivated me more than money." And to her credit, through the Covid-19 pandemic, Angie has not only been able to give back to local residents in her West Maui community, but she has continued to use proceeds of her business to support needy kids in El Salvador and twenty-three other countries through an organization called Compassion International.

As she told Alexa Nota in an interview for rentresponsiblity.org, "My whole focus is about giving back and using the blessing that we have to benefit others. That's always been my call: to encourage other small businesses and property management companies to consider how they can use what they've been given to help others.

Everyone's "why" for growth is different, but it is important to know what your "why" is and stay committed to it in the ups and downs you experience.

HELPFUL QUESTIONS TO ASK YOURSELF

Here is a little exercise I suggest you take before moving on to the next chapter.

Question 1: Rank the following reasons, in order of priority, for why you became a VRM.

1. To help others make meaningful memories

2. To invest and grow roots in the local community

3. To offer a unique accommodation experience better than staying in a hotel

4. To build a business and/or be your own boss

5. To find a better way to do vacation rental management

Question 2: Rank the following goals, in order of priority, for your VRM.

1. To build a profitable business

2. To be the best at delivering property management services to homeowners

3. To offer the best service and experience to guests

4. To provide the opportunity for others to experience and enjoy your location

5. To create a space for homeowners and guests to make their dreams a reality

Question 3: Rank the following strengths, in order of priority, of your VRM.

1. Revenue management

2. Guest services

3. Operations

4. Relationships with homeowners and guests

5. Local expertise and connections

Question 4: Rank the following reasons, in order of priority, for why it's important to grow your VRM.

1. To make a personal profit

2. To have the revenue to invest in improving guest services

3. To provide opportunities for the local community (jobs, tourism, etc.)

4. To have the revenue to strengthen business operations

5. To help more homeowners and guests enjoy the benefits of vacation rentals

Question 5: Rank the following challenges, in order of priority, when it comes to growing your VRM.

1. Not enough time

2. Lack of expertise

3. Minimal funds to allocate

4. Too much competition

5. Niche service offerings

This list is designed to provide clarity. When you know your "why," you are then in a place to focus on your "how."

2

PUSH THROUGH
GROWING PAINS

CHAPTER TWO

Push Through Growing Pains

"IT'S HARD. IT'S MEANT TO BE HARD. YOU'RE CHANGING THE WORLD."

– Tomasz Tunguz

To say there was much I did not know when I started would be an understatement. There were so many moving parts in building a vacation rental company that I hardly knew where to begin.

For starters, if you have anything to do with real estate in Maryland, you need a real estate broker's license. The only problem was this took three years to acquire, and it was only then we could submit our application. This was much longer than we were willing to wait. Thankfully, I found a local broker who was willing to assist us and our new brand. And while this transaction came at a steep cost, it was worth every penny because it meant we were in business.

Then there was the process of marketing our new company to homeowners. If you have no properties, you have no business. And for a new company this was difficult. Tack on top of that the challenge of finding the right homes to manage. As I like to say, your reputation as a VRM is only as good as the inventory you manage. If you have a property that has something wrong with it, you will get trashed on Yelp and other review sites, not because you are to blame, but because the owner failed to fix whatever problem there might be – such as an AC unit gone bad, poor paint job, or hard mattresses.

As one of my friends described it, being a VRM is kind of like trying to balance a teeter totter with the owner of the property sitting on one side and the guest on the other and you're standing in the middle.

When I first got started with Vantage Resort Realty, I did not realize how many touch points there would need to be with every guest interaction. After marketing, it might take ten inquiries just to book one or two reservations. Then, you had to send out a lodging agreement and process payment. When guests received this, they would often have questions and it was not uncommon for one guest to make upwards of ten calls. Start multiplying this across a growing list of properties and it was not long before this began to grow out of control.

Some guests were an absolute nightmare. I remember the early days we had this guy from New York who felt it was his life's duty to make everyone around him miserable. The house he was renting from us had a bit of an odd setup where the garage was asphalt. As a result, when customers walked in the door, they would end up tracking some of this on the carpet.

This prompted him to berate one of my guest services reps until the point he demanded to speak with me in person. It wasn't pretty and the confrontation grew so intense that I thought he might actually take a swing at me. Still, we wanted to do our best to make him happy and so we hired a local company to clean the carpets in his house, thinking this might solve the problem. But one hour later he was on the phone again, frustrated that the carpet was wet!

It's stories like this and others that left me to conclude running a vacation rental business is much like running a hotel – except all your rooms are in different locations and you don't own the inventory! You must make sure each unit is clean, properly inspected, up to code with state regulations, and well maintained. Very challenging to say the least!

Owning and operating a vacation rental company is a lot of work and there are a lot of growing pains that come with that job.

FIND SOMEONE TO HELP

The key to navigating these pains is finding some good people who help steer you in the right direction.

After I established a licensing agreement with our newfound broker, she took one look at my situation and knew I needed some help. She recommended I hire a lady named Darci that used to work for her, and said she could prove to be a real asset in helping me navigate some of the unknown. And as it turned out, she couldn't have been more right. Because I was new to this space, I needed someone to step in and show me the ropes. And to her credit, Darci knew the business well and this accelerated my understanding of the business by leaps and bounds.

My recommendation to anyone starting off in the vacation rental space is to find a mentor like Darci who has walked the road before them. If you don't know where to begin, VRMB.com with my friend Matt Landau is a terrific place to start. Another option is to get involved with one of the personal Mastermind groups I lead. Once a month, I get together with a few VRMs for just over an hour, and we go over certain challenges and opportunities.

As Vantage continued to grow, I began adding others to the team that had experience in the vacation rental space. This was a plus in many respects, but a glaring negative in others. Because so many of the other companies were doing it wrong, many of my early hires brought with them certain aspects of a faulty system.

More than once, I would hear one of them make a comment to me like, "Brooke, no other vacation rental business in Ocean City does it this way." And my response was always, "Exactly! That's the point. We're not like others in our space!"

In my mind, I knew if we were going to gain market share we needed to build a business that was completely different from the competition. Take this one small example: Until Vantage Resort Realty came on the scene, almost every rental in Ocean City was a Saturday-to-Saturday agreement. It didn't matter if a customer couldn't use three of those days. That was how it was always done, and thus was the only option available to customers.

But I decided to buck this trend and implemented "Flex-stays" that allowed homes to be rented out for dates of the guests' choosing, just like a traditional hotel. When I instituted this option, my team pushed back. "Brooke, if you do this, you're going to leave gaps and we are going to end up losing money."

But instead, just the opposite happened. Flex pricing was such a hit with customers that we ended up renting out homes for 30-40% above their previous listed value. Sure, there ended up being a few more gaps, but the extra money we made on the increased rates was worth it.

Again, growing pains.

THE MYTH OF BALANCE

One of the hardest parts of starting any new venture is the time and effort it takes and the tug it has on your personal life. Everyone talks about the importance of having a work and personal life balance, but the truth is, when you are a startup, it is an almost impossible challenge to navigate.

For the first five years of Vantage, I left my home in Baltimore every Monday at 5 a.m. and drove down to Ocean City till Friday at 4 p.m. During our ten-week peak season, it felt like I was drinking out of a firehose. I was the guy who would work a fourteen-hour day and then drop off linens to a location at 11 p.m. on a Saturday night.

Unless you have been in this position, it is hard to describe what this is like. As you grow, your workload increases, and you know you need to hire someone. The problem is you can't afford it and you get placed in this awkward position where you can't afford to hire someone, but you know you must grow. Going back to our Chapter One section with the five different personas, I am the Entrepreneur VRM to a T.

To me, everything is about growth. It is what motivates me to do what I do each day.

And yes, as you grow, the pace does become less frantic. But this does not diminish the real challenge it is in the early days to get off the ground. Some days, it was all overwhelming because I saw so many things that were wrong around me, but I did not have time to address them all.

Now, you might not be willing to make the sacrifices I made to achieve what I accomplished. That's okay. Everyone has their definition of success. For example, the average vacation rental company has sixty properties. That is a great number for many people! But for me, I knew I wanted to create something special that had never been done in our area before.

SHIFTING MY APPROACH

Soon after starting Vantage, I discovered I was a good marketer but not necessarily the best operator. I knew how to present a product and how to sell, but I struggled to build out the systems and processes required.

This adjustment brought with it a fresh series of growth pains. Even though I had led a successful company in the past, this space was still new to me and that transition from being a rookie in the space to being a mid-level industry leader brought a new set of challenges and a change in mindset.

As I often describe to others, business owners who are in the mid-level section are invested in the business full time. They have said goodbye to their former occupation, and they are "all-in." Post-it notes and physical calendars are no longer sufficient tools of the trade and must be replaced with the latest industry software that will allow them to effectively track their current customers and potential clients so none fall through the cracks. They start surrounding themselves with a team of qualified individuals who specialize in various aspects of the business.

In one sense, I was already at this position from day one. I was 100% committed. But even though my focus was clear, my understanding of the industry needed to evolve.

It meant I had to give up more control to my team. In the early days of Vantage, I was doing everything. I was the account manager, salesperson, and receptionist. In fact, my Sunday afternoon ritual in the offseason was to watch football with my family as we created personalized postcards, licked the stamps, and sent them out to potential customers (every child's dream!). But as we grew, I recognized the need to shift roles. I had to stop taking on every responsibility and focus my time on being an ambassador for our brand.

As our company expanded to over fifty properties, I had to make yet another shift and take my leadership to the next level. The growing pains never stopped.

BIG COMPANIES WANT TO SQUASH YOU

One of the reasons I would challenge you to grow and remain on your toes is because there are giants in the vacation rental sector that want to squash every competitor that stands in their way.

Many of these large venture capital conglomerates are flush with cash and have no choice but to grow. They must provide a solid return for their investors. To many, they are seen as the evil empire because they are big corporations who care little about individual communities and are solely focused on the bottom line. They are the stormtroopers of Star Wars and are out to destroy all that stands in their path.

Of course, I am being a bit facetious. It's not as though companies such as Vacasa, Turnkey (recently bought out by Vacasa), Evolve, and others are evil just because they want to make money; but it is important to note the impact they have on this space. Like it or not, when you step into the vacation rental industry, you are competing with giants like this that seek a monopoly. Part of their success is your failure.

Pile on the rise of non-traditional platforms like Airbnb, and this only adds to your competition. Even locations that were previously seen as non-vacation rental areas now provide opportunities for guests to rent. The market has reached a whole new level of saturation.

I say this not to discourage you, but to motivate you to put your head down and grind it out. Competition is on the rise, and to keep ahead of the game you must be all in. Yes, there will be growing pains. Still, these will be worth it in the end because of the tremendous opportunity the vacation rental space provides.

To understand this opportunity, you must first grasp a basic, yet revolutionary concept called the real value of inventory.

3

THE VALUE OF
INVENTORY

CHAPTER THREE

The Value of Inventory

If you have no inventory, you have no business. It's as simple as that. Sometimes I work with people who say, "Brooke, I want to expand my business and take it to the level just like you did with Vantage."

My response always starts with a question. "How many properties do you have?" Not how many properties they want to have or how many properties they *plan* to have, but how many properties they *currently* have in their portfolio.

When you have inventory, obtaining guests becomes easy. You take the properties you have, place them on various marketing channels, and you are good to go. But the hardest part is getting the inventory itself.

For example, I have a partner (we call our customers partners) in Boston who wanted to launch a new venture seventy miles away in Cape Cod. But several months into this process, and he was stuck. His flywheel had ground to a halt, and he found himself with zero properties and in a desperate financial situation.

After coming alongside to assess his situation, I deduced the major problem – his brand did not resonate with his target clientele! He was taking his Boston company approach and trying to force it into the community of Cape Cod. And as close as these two places were on the map, the residents of each location were very different.

As a result, we had to start over from scratch. We created a new name, designed a new website, developed a fresh target list, created a unique selling proposition, built out key features and benefits that differentiated his company, and sent out postcards to spread the word. Before long, his business turned around and he went from someone who was on the verge of giving up to someone who developed a prosperous business.

Without inventory, his business was nothing more than a name. But with inventory he now had a platform from which to grow.

THE TRUE VALUE OF INVENTORY

One of the discoveries I have made is that few business owners in the vacation rental space know the real value of one of their properties. I was a corporate finance major in college and so I grasped this concept naturally. But other people do not, and struggle to be strategic long-term thinkers.

While everyone uses different terminology, for purposes of clarity let's stick with a simple illustration. First, let's look at the average value of return on one vacation rental property. After speaking with hundreds of VRMs, I have come to see the average gross booking revenue always ends up being right around $36,000 per property. Some are more, and some are less, but the average always tends to fall in this range. I've seen aggregate reports across thousands of properties and over a billion in gross reservations and again, the average has historically been around $36,000 per property per year.

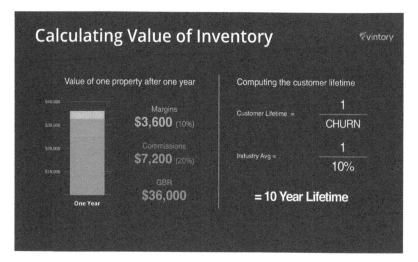

I've also seen the average vacation rental company charge around 20% commission. This means that on a $36,000 property you can expect to make $7,200 in commissions per year. After EBITA (earnings before interest, taxes, and amortization), your net sales for the year will come in at approximately 10% of the gross booking revenue. So, for a $36,000 property, you could expect to net $3,600 in profit – a fantastic return.

The key is to create a business that is sustainable. Short-term rentals and other recurring revenue businesses are different from many companies because the revenue for the service comes over an extended period – the lifetime of the customer. If a customer is happy with the service, they will likely stick around for a long time, and the profit that can be made from that customer will increase considerably. On the other hand, if a customer is unhappy, they will churn quickly, and the business will lose money on the investment they made to acquire that customer.

This creates a fundamentally different dynamic to that of a traditional business. For every vacation home rental, there are essentially two sales that must be made:

- Sale 1: Getting a homeowner to sign up for your rental program

- Sale 2: Keeping that same homeowner happy

The more I think about it, the more I appreciate this model of doing business because it creates a culture of authentic accountability. You have to continue to deliver value to the customer, continue to innovate, continue to execute or they will fire you. It's the optimal customer/ vendor relationship.

Now, it's important to point out that you are always going to lose a certain percentage of clients due to the natural churn rate in every organization. But keep in mind your inventory is critical to your success and you must do all you can to maximize your inventory expansion and minimize its turnover.

One of the ways you can do this is by taking note of your churn rate over the span of two to three years and then calculate your annual average. If you have a hundred properties, you need to know if you are losing five, ten, or twenty a year. It's simple math but if you are bringing in ten new properties a year while losing ten in the process, you are treading water.

Know the true value your inventory holds.

LIFETIME VALUE

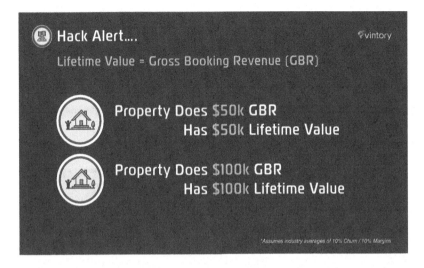

From my experience, the average lifespan of a vacation rental unit is ten years. Multiply the net value of an average property ($3,600) times ten and you arrive at the number we started with in our previous illustration – $36,000.

This is simple when you think about it. Know your yearly gross booking revenue on a property and you will have a solid estimate for the amount you will make on the lifetime of that same property. Margins times number of years equals lifetime value. As the old saying goes, we overestimate what we can do in a year, but we underestimate what can take place in a decade!

Knowing this lifetime value should change our approach. For example, many business owners in the vacation home rental market will gulp if a realtor requests a $500 referral fee for a new property. But in doing so, this business owner loses sight of the property's lifetime value. If over the span of ten years they make $36,000, spending $500 or even $2,000 is nothing in comparison to the long-term value they receive.

At Vintory we have an outsourced business development unit that hires us to go out and get contracts. These VRM's pay us 25% of the gross booking revenue. Sticking with our $36,000 model, this comes out to an average of $9,000 per contract. To them, even though this cuts into 2.5 years of profits they make on this property, they will take this deal every day of the week because they know they will continue to make income on this unit from years 2.5-10. This is why I always remind business owners I coach that their lifetime value comes from having consistent inventory.

The fastest way you can grow your vacation rental business is by adding new properties to your portfolio. Think about it. If you add ten properties this year, you are adding an average of $360K in profit over the lifetime of your business. And keep in mind that even though I give the rule of thumb of first year margins times number of years, there is a thing called inflation.

I own a vacation rental in Bethany Beach, Delaware. When I first started renting it close to a decade ago, I was happy with $16,000 in rental income per year. However, the past three years I've done over $70,000! Most vacation rentals increase over time, thus increasing the lifetime value of a property.

I like to think of each property I manage as one big pile of money. When I do this and see what I will make on average with this property in the coming years, it clarifies any additional expenses I might have to make.

VALUE AT EXIT

Exciting as all this is, there is still an important piece of the puzzle missing. Not only do you make money every year you have a property in your rental portfolio, but you also make an additional profit the day you sell your business. My friend Matt Landau with VRMB.com likes to say, "Build your vacation rental business as though you will own it forever but could sell it tomorrow."[32]

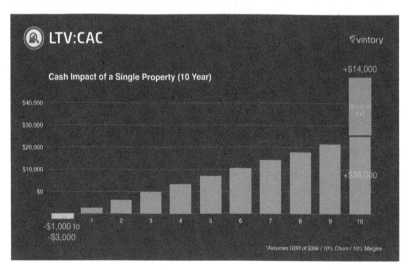

Keep in mind that the vast majority of the value of your company is the management contracts you hold. The average management company is usually sold between three to five times its yearly net profit. Sticking with our $3,600 illustration, if we multiply this number times three,

[32] https://mattlandau.wistia.com/medias/db0cqg76eb

we find ourselves with $10,800. Multiply it by five and we have $18,000. Sometimes the profit margins are even higher. For example, at Vintory we have an outsourced business development division where we sell contracts for as much as $25,000 or greater.

All of this means that if you have an average successful vacation rental business for over ten years, you can expect to net $36,000 in total recurring revenue from the property itself and then an additional $10,800 to $18,000 on each property when you sell those rights to a prospective buyer. You are essentially double dipping into the profit pool.

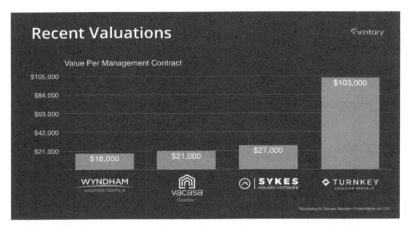

There are multiple other examples that show the value of inventory at exit including: Vacasa's acquisition of Wyndham for $18,000/contract, or Sykes acquisition by Vitruvian Partners for $27,000. Even Vacasa's investor deck showed they paid on average $21,000/contract through their corporate development efforts. With all of that said, there isn't a better example than Vacasa's acquisition of TurnKey. In early March of 2021, they purchased their competitor for $619 million.[33] At the time of the sale, Vacasa had approximately 24,000 rental units and TurnKey

---

33   https://skift.com/2021/11/30/vacasa-paid-619-million-for-turnkey-vacation-rentals-in-mostly-stock/

had 6,000.[34] This meant that TurnKey made $103,000 per door through this final sale transaction! BOOM!

> **Want to know what your company is worth? Check out Vintory's interactive company valuation calculator at Vintory.com/calculators/company-valuation-calculator or vintory.com/valuation**

The bottom line is this: Each management contract you have is super valuable not only as an annuity but also as an asset you can sell. This is one of the reasons I am so passionate about this industry!

INCREASING YOUR INVENTORY SHOULD EXCITE YOU

At the end of the day, I am a finance guy. I readily admit it doesn't take much to get me excited when I see numbers like the ones I have outlined. But even people who detest numbers should find this exciting. And all of this data should challenge you to make expanding your inventory a top priority.

Imagine how your bottom line could increase if you grew your business by even a few properties this coming year. As I often say, there isn't a better return on your investment in our industry than adding more inventory!

---

34   https://shorttermrentalz.com/news/vacasa-final-turnkey-acquisition/

4

INVENTORY METRICS

CHAPTER FOUR

Inventory Metrics

"IF YOU CANNOT MEASURE IT, YOU CANNOT IMPROVE IT."

— Lord Kelvin

The very name of our company, Vintory, gives you a clue as to the value I place on vacation rental inventory. I think it is so important that I made up a word and based an entire company around it! (Also, it didn't hurt that spell check always changed "vintory" to "victory.")

In the previous chapter I outlined the real value of inventory and how adding just a handful of properties can dramatically increase your bottom line. To summarize: if you do not grow your inventory, you will not make it very far. This is a message I will continue to repeat.

Many property owners become consumed in the day-to-day operations and put inventory on the back burner. This often means owner acquisition strategies fall to the side. But by doing some analysis of inventory metrics, we are able to better understand what it costs to acquire a new property and how much we can net off each property we acquire, otherwise known as unit economics.

KNOW YOUR CUSTOMER ACQUISITION COSTS

Sometimes the whole business of acquiring new homeowners feels like a daunting challenge and it is hard to know where to start. But whenever I feel this way, I go back to those words from Lord Kelvin, "If you cannot measure it, you cannot improve it."

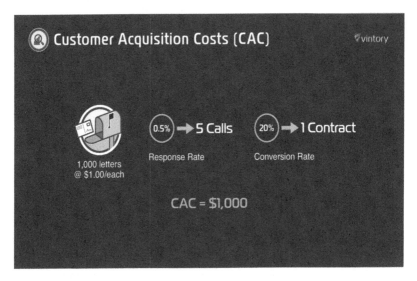

You must know your customer acquisition cost (CAC). How much does it cost you to acquire a new owner? When I ask this question to many vacation rental managers, they often stare back at me with a blank expressions on their faces. Even many successful vacation rental managers who have been in the industry for decades still do not know an estimate of what it costs them to acquire new inventory. They have a basic idea in the back of their minds, but they cannot produce a hard number.

So, to clear up any confusion and make this picture as clear as possible, let's use a basic illustration. Say you send out a thousand postcards that cost you $1 a card. This means your marketing spend is $1,000. According to the Direct Marketing Association, the average response rate on direct mail is 0.5%. Assuming you hit this number, you now have a grand total of five inbound leads. Of those five leads, let's say you close 20% of the potential deals, netting you one owner. In summary, for that $1,000 you spent in marketing, you were able to acquire one new customer. Therefore, your customer acquisition cost is $1,000.

On the surface, this might seem like a high price to pay, but if your first-year margins are $3,600 this investment is a no-brainer. Keeping in mind the average vacation rental homeowner remains with one company for anaverage of ten years, your long-term rate of return will be well worth the cost of those one thousand postcards.

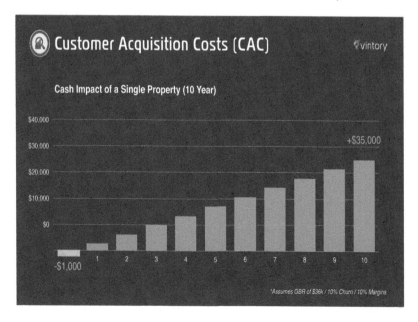

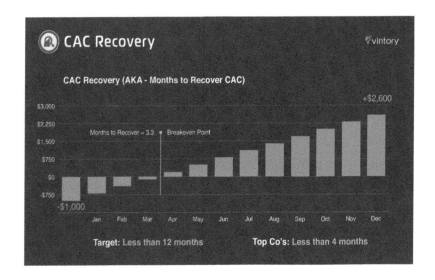

Again, with my finance background, this process is second nature to me. Know your CAC and then determine how many months of profits it takes to pay back your marketing investment. From an industry perspective, if you keep your CAC under twelve months revenue, you are in great shape. Some of the best companies get their CAC in under four months.

Regardless, it is a common fact that the most successful VRMs know their opportunity cost and they focus on making decisions that generate the greatest long-term value.

I strongly believe that as a VRM, you need to focus on making investments in your company to grow, and this belief took me from 0 to 500 properties in just five years.

THE MOST IMPORTANT NUMBER TO TRACK

The basics of unit economics is calculating how much you make from every dollar you invest. This leads us to the Holy Grail of all metrics acquisition – the LTV to CAC ratio. The LTV:CAC ratio is my favorite metric because it takes into account all of the key factors in one simple number: profit margins, churn, and acquisition costs. And if your mind is starting to drift a bit, stick with me. The good stuff is coming!

Going back to that illustration from the previous chapter where we look at each property as one big pile of money, we have to ask ourselves how much of the pile we get to keep. The basic way we do this is by determining the lifetime value (LTV) of a property and then dividing by our customer acquisition costs (CAC).

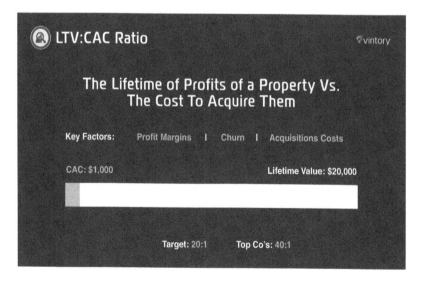

If you have a property that makes $20,000 over the span of ten years and it costs you $1,000 to acquire it, you have a LTV:CAC Ratio of 20. Said another way – you invested $1,000 and brought in $20,000, thus netting you $19,000.

Even if you are not a numbers nerd like me, if there is

one metric for inventory acquisition you need to know, this is the one.

For average companies, their LTV is twenty times greater than their CAC while top companies make as much as forty times their CAC. This means that on a property that costs them $2,000 to acquire, they are making anywhere between $40,000 – $80,000.

If you have a solid LTV:CAC ratio, and a systematic way of getting new properties, back up a truck of cash, and invest it back into your business, because you have a money-making machine!

This takes us to another important point – margins. One of the first questions I ask new clients of Vintory is, "What are your margins?" Yet again, this is often met with a blank stare along with a few wild estimates.

But the way you discover your profit margin is very simple. You start by determining what you made last year and then determining your total top line gross booking revenue. After speaking with hundreds of vacation rental managers, this number usually comes out to around 10%. This means that a property with a gross booking revenue of $36,000 will have an approximate margin of $3,600. Please note, this is before taxes, fees, insurance, etc., otherwise known as "owner rent."

Along with this, you must take into account your annual churn rate. What percentage of your portfolio is no longer with you this year? How many properties did you lose last year? How many did you lose the year before that? And so forth.

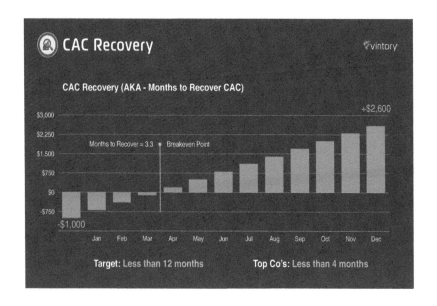

SHIFT YOUR MINDSET TO HELP PEOPLE WIN

The more you understand the data behind inventory metrics the more you will have a lasting change in mindset. You will take customer acquisition seriously, and develop a strong data target list. You will focus your energy on hitting the right customers who will be the perfect fit for your business. Your approach to referrals will change you, and you will develop a strong network that can help your business succeed.

This mindset shift is getting out of the rut of ordinary thinking and replacing it with a mindset that will take your business to the next level. You stop small-minded thinking and open yourself up to greater opportunities. You won't think twice about rewarding a realtor for helping you secure a new property because you have created a win-

win situation. And instead of trying to squeeze every last drop of profit out of the properties you have, you go out and acquire ten new ones and maximize your growth in the process.

You are moving from survive to thrive mode. And as you do this, it is amazing how others will begin to notice and have more confidence in your business. As you provide value for individuals such as realtors, they will want to give you their business to return the favor.

At the end of the day, it's all about doing business the right way. You are treating others the way you would want to be treated. When you find a new owner, instead of telling them all that you can do for them, you are pausing to listen for their unique pain points. You hear the concerns they have and the goals they want to accomplish and then come up with a game plan to help them achieve those goals.

NUMBERS POINT TO STORIES

Numbers are powerful because behind every number is a story. I cannot tell you how many people have walked up to me after a conference or interview and said something to this effect, "Brooke, I have been in this industry for decades, but I never sat down and did the math to figure out where my business was at. Thank you!"

Not long ago, my good buddy Jason Sprenkle and I were at a conference together and after looking out at the scores of people in attendance Jason remarked to me, "What happened to our little industry?!"

Sometimes I wonder that very question myself. When I look back at how different the vacation rental space was in 2007, I am astounded by how much it has changed. Every year there are thousands of new vacation rental managers who are eager to experience the same growth I experienced during my days with Vantage. And rather than seeing them as more competition, I have taken on the role of a cheerleader. I want to see them succeed!

Just like me in the early days of my business, these young entrepreneurs do not always know where to start and how to get their flywheel moving. They see all the huge vacation rental conglomerations and think to themselves, "I can't compete with that!"

But this is where I get chills down my spine because it really is a David versus Goliath matchup. It's the behemoth giants against the little guys. And this is one of the primary reasons I started Vintory. Through our organization, we can bring a Venture Capital-like mindset to the average mom and pop shop and set people up to win by capitalizing on all they have to offer. This allows them to compete in such a way that even the big guys can't match!

IT'S TIME TO START

There has never been a time like the present to start growing your inventory. Our market is exploding, and coming out of Covid I already see a rise in growth.

When 2021 vacation bookings began, it was widely reported that vacation rental sites like Airbnb and VRBO were seeing a boom in bookings. Now the surge in demand for vacation rentals is so high, the short-term vacation rental industry has never seen occupancy rates at this level. All of this is leaving vacation rental managers to scramble to find more properties to rent out for available occupancy in a desperate attempt to help more families book their long-awaited vacations.

The lack of vacation rental inventory means bookings will become nearly impossible for many as travelers opt to choose the safety, security, and accommodations that rentals offer.

There has also never been more investment and acquisition activity in the industry. Simply put, there is more money, more interest, more demand, and more competition than ever before.

Now is the time to grow your inventory and to take advantage of these trends while they last.

The market has exploded. Why can't your business?

5

MAKE A PLAN

CHAPTER FIVE

Make a Plan

> "THE BEST WAY TO PREDICT YOUR FUTURE IS TO CREATE YOUR FUTURE."
>
> — Abraham Lincoln

As the old saying goes, the difference between a dream and a goal is a plan. From day one of your vacation rental business, you need to know what you want to accomplish and lay out a game plan for how you will get there.

When I started Vantage Resort Realty, there were parts of the business beyond my understanding. I was the rookie to a brand-new game. But from the first day I started Vantage, I knew where I wanted to take the company. I didn't want to settle and just earn a living. I wanted to create something special.

Even though there were numerous points where my game plan had to be adjusted, I knew where I wanted to go and had a good idea of how to get there. I knew that bringing in a lot of properties was going to be no small challenge and would require intense focus. Because I knew where I wanted to go, I was willing to make the necessary sacrifices to make this dream a reality.

Creating a plan eliminates the guesswork and keeps you focused on what you need to do to get where you want to go.

RICHES IN NICHES

"INCH WIDE, MILE DEEP."

– Strava co-founder Mark Gainey

The first step in creating a plan is to find your niche. To compete in a competitive arena, you need to focus on your specific market.

Ask yourself, "What kind of inventory do I want?" Do you only want waterfront properties, ski-in/ski-out properties, a certain number of bedroom homes, or golf course properties? All of these are viable options, but this is where you need to know your market and the skills you bring to the table. What excites you? Where is there untapped potential that your competitors are not capitalizing on?

Then, after you know the type of inventory you want, focus on being the best at this niche you can possibly be. This is different for every VRM.

For instance, there is a company called First Flight Rentals in Outer Banks, North Carolina. They are in a bit of an odd market that is known for its incredibly large vacation rental homes. Ten, twenty, and even thirty-bedroom homes are just part of the norm for that area. Rather than focusing on this same market and facing tons of competition, First

Flight decided they would set their sights only on condos. They let all the other companies in their area chase the large home and they focused on their niche. In the process, they have created a strong, sustainable company.

IDENTIFY YOUR GOALS

After you have found your niche and know the approximate size of your market, you are able to set some attainable goals to move the needle. I stress attainable because few things are worse than setting a goal that is beyond your ability to achieve. You have to know how many properties you can onboard and have a budget in place for your rise in CAC costs.

If you are currently at one hundred vacation rental properties, do not expect to move to five hundred in six months. It takes time and if you move too quickly you run the risk of the wheels falling off the cart and doing more harm than good.

Instead, know where you want to go, dig into the numbers, and then set an ambitious but realistic goal. If you are at a hundred properties and want to be at 140, create a plan to get there. Start with your churn rate. If you are losing ten properties on an annual basis, this means that you will need to add fifty units of inventory to your portfolio if you want to reach your goal this coming year.

I have stressed the churn rate several times because I have noticed a recent uptick in these numbers over the past year due to COVID. Many homeowners have decided to make their vacation house their permanent residence.

Others have seen a rise in property valuations and have decided to sell.

Even if your strategy needs to be adjusted to match the broader changes in culture, keep coming back to your goal. Know what you want to achieve and eliminate excuses that stand in your way.

CREATE YOUR GAME PLAN

After you have identified your goals, it's time to create a game plan. Sticking with our previous illustration, if you have a hundred properties and know you need to add fifty, you need a strategy to get there.

For example, you might decide to add twenty-five properties through direct mail, ten through referrals, and fifteen through inbound or digital. That's great and certainly doable. But let's just take the first part of this equation. To add twenty-five properties through direct mail, you will need to send out around 5,500 postcards. If each postcard costs a dollar, you are looking at spending $220 to acquire each new property.

We have created this terrific interactive calculator that allows you to calculate all of your metrics. Find it here: www.vintory.com/calculators/roi-estimator

Notice what we are doing with each step. We are eliminating the guesswork and creating a plan. And when you eliminate the guesswork, you eliminate the excuses.

Adding twenty-five new pieces of inventory might seem daunting. But sending out 5,500 postcards is doable.

In summary, creating a game plan is simplified when you break it into manageable chunks.

THINK KAIZEN

Back in July of 2010, I decided to compete in my first Ironman triathlon. This all started up in Lake Placid, New York, when I watched my friend Tim complete his Ironman and was inspired by what I saw. Everyone started at 7 a.m. and the cut off was midnight. By that point, each participant was to have swum 2.4 miles, completed a 112-mile bike ride, and run a full marathon of 26.2 miles.

What inspired me most was when the clock neared midnight. Almost all of the participants, including those who had finished earlier on in the day, came to the finish line to cheer on those who were just completing the course. I found myself in tears as I watched determined people struggle to cross and, in that moment, I knew this was something I wanted to do.

There was only one tiny problem; I was in terrible physical shape! And as soon as that thought of being an Ironman crossed my mind, it was immediately canceled out with another thought that said, "Brooke, who are you kidding? You never ran, biked, or swam close to any of those distances. There is no chance you will ever be able to accomplish this!"

This almost led me to give up on the idea, but that was when an old Japanese approach called Kaizen came to my mind. For those who are unfamiliar with this term, Kaizen is the art of achieving small incremental improvements – it literally means "change for the better." It has been used by hundreds of top global organizations to create an environment of continuous improvement.

With this thought in mind, I set a goal and signed up for the Baltimore Half Marathon that October. And let me just say that I started out small. Here's an example of how I used Kaizen to begin my training:

- Day 1: Research running shoes.
- Day 2: Find running store to buy shoes.
- Day 3: Buy shoes.
- Day 4: Try on shoes and stand on the treadmill. Seriously. Just stand on the treadmill.
- Day 5: Walk on treadmill for ten minutes.
- Day 6: Walk on the treadmill for five minutes. Jog for one minute. Walk for four minutes.
- Day 7: Walk on the treadmill for five minutes. Jog for five minutes. Walk for five minutes.

There is nothing revolutionary about any of these steps! And if you have never used an approach like this, it might seem a little bizarre. But I can assure you it works! Using this method, I completed the Baltimore Half Marathon.

Next came the most challenging task – swimming. I knew if I was ever going to compete in a triathlon, I needed to learn how to swim. Going back to the Kaizen approach, I found a pool in my area and began taking lessons. For you who are squeamish at heart, I will spare you the details. But let's just say that the first day was anything but spectacular and ended with me throwing up in the changing room. It was humiliating and the voices of doubt began to creep back into my head.

By that point, though, I was committed. I stuck with it and continued to practice every day. Before long, I signed up for the shortest triathlon I could find. Not long after that, I stepped up my game and completed my first half Ironman – a 1.2-mile swim, 56-mile bike ride, followed by a 13.1-mile run.

I felt great and knew I was ready to train the big one. Still, I had one more obstacle to face – selling this idea to my wife. Signing up for an Ironman is a huge family commitment. You spend much of your free time training and a five-to-six-hour bike ride is par for the course. But my wife supported me, and I signed up for Ironman Florida 2013. Looking back, I couldn't have even attempted this goal without all the support she provided, and it taught me a great lesson on the importance of surrounding yourself with positive people.

True to the Kaizen approach, I laid out my schedule week by week, day by day, for the entire year. Come race day and I was set to go. I knew my goals for each phase, and I had my nutrition planned almost to the minute.

I knew the run was going to be the toughest part and that 18-26.2-mile stretch was going to be the killer. There is the reason they call this section "the walk of the zombies" because it is so easy to hit a mental wall where you do not want to take another step forward.

But when I got to that point, instead of focusing on the pain my body felt, I made a game out of it and set a goal to pass one hundred participants during this stretch. I passed

170. And while there were others who started the race that were more athletic than me, many of them gave up along the way – not because they were incapable of doing what I was doing, but because they did not have a clear-cut game plan to succeed.

On that day, I executed my plan to perfection and hit my goals in almost every phase. I wasn't fast, but I finished and that was my goal. And for the rest of my life, I now hold that coveted title – Ironman!

WHAT MY IRONMAN TRAINING TAUGHT ME

"A GOAL SHOULD SCARE YOU A LITTLE, AND EXCITE YOU A LOT."

– Dr. Joe Vitale

This whole Ironman training taught me several things and showed me that anyone can accomplish any goal they set out to achieve so long as they:

1. Write their goal down on paper

2. Make the plan

3. Surround themselves with good people

4. Work their butt off

Chances are, since you are reading this book, you are committed to building your business the right way. You want to avoid some of the common pitfalls that I and others in this industry have slipped into along the way.

Let me just urge you to affirm your commitment by putting it on paper. Write down two or three goals you have for your business. Where would you like to see yourself in five years? Do you want to build a business you can sell to others? Do you want to set up a long-term sustainable stream of residual revenue that will bring you and your family multi-generational wealth?

Know where you want to go, make a plan, and then take small incremental steps to arrive at your target destination.

6

GETTING THE RIGHT
PEOPLE IN THE RIGHT
SEATS

CHAPTER SIX

Getting the Right People in the Right Seats

"IT DOESN'T MAKE SENSE TO HIRE SMART PEOPLE AND THEN TELL THEM WHAT TO DO; WE HIRE SMART PEOPLE SO THEY CAN TELL US WHAT TO DO."

— Steve Jobs

"HIRE YOUR WEAKNESSES AS SOON AS YOU CAN AFFORD TO."

— Sara Blakey at Spanx

When you have a solid plan, it will not be long before you start to grow. This is where your business can take on some new challenges. As you enter the height of the vacation rental season from Memorial Day to Labor Day, your regular schedule will expand to twelve-hour days and your inbox will be filled with emails. Trust me, it will be all you can do just to keep up!

In the early days, you might be in a place where you can do everything. But if you continue to scale, you need to bring others on board and have them share the load. If you are an owner and you continue to take care of everything on your own, you are missing out on opportunities you might not even know exist.

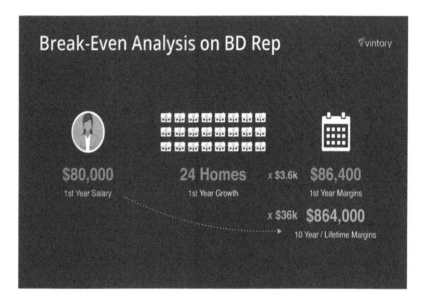

Let's say, for instance, it costs you $80,000 a year to bring on someone who can dedicate themselves to inventory acquisition. That might seem like a high number at first, but when you run the numbers, this figure begins to make a lot more sense.

Using this $80,000 example, let's say you hire someone who is slightly below average, and they bring in only two new pieces of inventory each month. This means that at the end of the year you have twenty-four new properties. Again, assuming the average gross booking revenue is $36,000 and your average net figure is 10% of this number, this means your year-end total will be twenty-four properties times $3,600 – which brings you to a grand total of $86,400.

This means in year one you have more than broken even on this hire. But here is where it gets even better. Because the new business they have brought in will remain in your portfolio for an average of ten years, not only have they paid for themselves in year one, but they have potentially covered their salary for the next ten years!

Now, keep in mind this process is not always this straightforward. You might have to borrow money for this initial hire, and it will take some time before you recoup your investment. Plus, if you pick the wrong person, you can end up losing more money than you gain.

This is why it is critical that you hire the right people.

IT'S ALL ABOUT THE TEAM

"IF YOU WANT TO GO FAST, GO ALONE. IF YOU WANT TO GO FAR, GO TOGETHER."

– African Proverb

After twenty years of running my own businesses, I have come to realize that growing a great team is the key to building a successful company. Before your business grows, you need to know the types of people you want onboard.

Finding the right team member can make all the difference. One person who does their job with excellence can be ten times more valuable than ten average employees. The contrast is also true and one "virus employee" can corrupt even the most loyal team.

But as a business leader in a growing organization, hiring must become your number one responsibility. As the founder of Vintory, my three main responsibilities include casting vision, hiring people, and building culture. Approximately two-thirds of my job revolves around adding to and building our team.

Even though our organization has grown significantly, and we now have over fifty people on our team, I make it a point to personally interview every candidate for every position. This is how important hiring is to us.

Internally, I know that as our team grows we will continue to reproduce what we already are. In other words, if we have a team that is built poorly on a small scale, we will continue this trend as we grow. If we have one lazy worker on a team of ten, this means that ten percent of our company is underperforming. If this trend continues unchecked, as we grow to a hundred, our number of poor employees will grow to ten. This will create no shortage of problematic situations.

I often say one of the greatest benefits we can give members of our organization is to raise up a team of people who actually care about what they do. Having colleagues that are highly motivated, driven, and focused is the greatest business perk you can offer.

THE RIGHT PEOPLE IN THE RIGHT SEATS

As Jim Collins' book *Good to Great* reminds us, you need the right people on the bus, and you need the right people sitting in the right seats. There have been a few hires I made where I knew the person I brought on board was a winner. However, I wasn't sure where they would fit. I just knew they were going along for the journey.

Early on in my career as a leader in the mortgage industry, I was unrefined in my hiring process and ended up bringing on several people who were poor fits. Sure, I had this team of a hundred people, but there were always around ten to fifteen percent of our group that were not fully on board.

Even when I switched over to Vantage and started hiring my first few team members, I look back and realize some of the success I had can be attributed to nothing more than raw luck!

Take for example my friend Denny. When we first met, he had zero experience in the vacation rental space. But we got along great, he interviewed well, and I knew I wanted him on the bus. Even though I was confident he would be a success, I had no idea how much he would thrive in his new role. He absolutely killed it and to date has personally signed up over 400 management contracts.

Not long after Denny was hired, I implemented a psychometric personality assessment as part of our hiring process at Vantage. Through this assessment, I identified five primary profiles that were just what we needed: Persuaders, Trailblazers, Rainmakers, Captains, and Mavericks.

Out of curiosity, I asked Denny to take the assessment and he fit perfectly into one of the categories. He was a Trailblazer. And in that moment, things began to click for me. Through using this little personality profile hack, I quit the guessing game and knew with relative certainty the kinds of people I needed to add to my team.

Over the past ten years, I have been using psychometric personality assessments and it has been the number one reason for our success. I often joke that it is so good it feels like we're cheating!

PSYCHOMETRIC PERSONALITY ASSESSMENTS

There are a couple of different psychometric personality assessments available. Some prefer what are called Predictive Index assessments, but others prefer Culture

Index.[32] The Culture Index we use has eighteen typified patterns that are broken down into four categories:

Category 1 is the visionary and includes people who are classified as daredevils, philosophers, architects, enterprisers, and trailblazers.

Category 2 is the technical person and is composed of individuals who are referred to as technical experts, scholars, specialists, and craftsmen.

Category 3 highlights social patterns and represents people who are persuaders, rainmakers, operators, and traditionalists.

Category 4 takes us to organizational individuals. These are your administrators, coordinators, facilitators, operators, and traditionalists.

Personally, I fall into the Daredevil category. I am keen to take risks, start new ventures, and keep moving forward. I don't spend a lot of time worried about the past and I am always looking for the next mountain to climb. It is this mindset that drove me to launch several companies and take on audacious personal challenges such as attempting an Ironman.

The type of profile I look for in others all depends on the position I need fulfilled. Soon after I exited Vantage, I took a job in Orlando as a chief business development officer. By that point, I realized how important psychometric assessments were and knew I needed to hire someone who was a Persuader. Along came this guy named Brian and we hit it off almost immediately. Still, I needed to know where he fit on the spectrum.

4   https://www.cultureindex.com/

After running him through this assessment, to my delight he scored as a 94% match for our business development role and he was a Persuader – someone who was venturesome, enthusiastic, driving, and tolerant of uncertainty. That was the confirmation I needed, and we hired him that week. To date, Brian has signed up more luxury vacation rental home contracts in the city of Orlando than anyone I know.

Culture Index surveys are powerful, and they get you 70% of the way across the hiring finish line. That said, there is still work to be done.

RIGHT PERSON, WRONG SEAT

There have been times when I walked into a situation and found that we had the wrong person on the bus. There were no other options at that point. They needed to go. But I usually find we have the right person in the wrong seat.

Take for example the illustration of Mike and Alicia. Mike was in a business development role and everyone in the company was fond of him. He was detail oriented but struggled to get contracts signed. Unfortunately, his attention to the minutia meant he talked potential customers out of deals rather than into them.

When I ran him through our Culture Index survey, I discovered Mike was a Craftsman with characteristics such as accommodating, analytical, deliberate, and precise. While I love Craftsmen (in fact, my daughter is a Craftsman!), it was clear that the role Mike was currently in did not call for someone with this personality. It needed someone who would bring in sales.

As it turned out, Mike was not the only person who was in the wrong seat. There was another individual on the team, Alicia, who was also having her own set of struggles. When I ran her through this same index, I discovered Alicia was a Rainmaker. And what do Rainmakers do? They make it rain! They are self-confident, persuasive, stimulating, fast paced, and informal.

After comparing notes, I swapped Mike and Alicia and placed them in roles where they would thrive. As a result, their productivity went through the roof, and they became outstanding members of the team.

We had the right people. We just needed them to sit in the right seats!

TOP THREE PERSONALITIES YOU NEED TO ACQUIRE INVENTORY

In regard to acquiring inventory, there are three primary Cultural Index profiles that are a perfect fit for business development and growth – Persuaders, Trailblazers, and Rainmakers. These are people who have a high sense of urgency that can border on annoying. They are passionate and driven but they struggle with the details.

Persuaders are proactive, impatient, and charismatic communicators. They are effective salespeople and sell themselves before they sell their product. They can be impatient and on the go. Persuaders know how to speak to people at their level. They know who they are selling to and adapt their personality to that of others. They are good at asking questions and listening.

Personally, if you have a steady stream of inbound leads coming in, go with a Persuader. Brian Riggs on my team is someone who fits this to a T. After experiencing some strong success in inventory acquisitions in Orlando, he became my business partner and co-founder at Vintory. He is such a great persuader because it is who he is. He is driven and wakes up every morning with a fire in his belly that says, "I've got to win!" He is socially comfortable, and unafraid to talk to anybody. All this makes him a natural salesperson.

Trailblazers are a little different. They are proactive, confident self-starters that thrive in competitive situations. They are focused on winning and are more analytical in their style of thinking. They can be impatient and restless. To some, this person can seem confusing and that they are all over the map.

Trailblazers are productive and thrive in competitive situations. They are focused on winning, analytical, driven, and can be sent into uncharted waters to tackle new territory. They can be very charming and great listeners. If you need someone to build a network of leads, Trailblazers are the way to go. Like the Persuader, they are driven to win and succeed. They are not sloppy, but they do not have a lot of attention to detail.

Rainmakers are the life of the party. They are extroverts and do well in social circles. They think out loud as they speak. They are optimistic and persuasive. Often, they struggle with details and keeping commitments to such an extent that others think they are lazy or uncommitted.

It's rare that Rainmakers stand on their own. They need a strong support person behind them who will keep them in check and clean up any messes they might make! Count on them to bring in a ton of new leads but do not depend on them to fill out an expense report!

Persuaders, Trailblazers, and Rainmakers. These are the three personality types you need to acquire inventory.

INTERVIEWS AND REFERRALS

In addition to a psychometric personality assessment, you need to conduct a series of strong interviews and collect some solid referrals.

Through this process, you want to discover those things an assessment might not tell you. What makes this person tick? What motivates them? How responsive are they? Do they pay attention to detail? What roles do they struggle in and where do they excel?

While psychometric personality assessments do a great job of finding someone's personality, they cannot measure such things such as social skills, how someone will respond under pressure, or someone's work ethic.

Take my brother, for instance, who is a real-life architect. Chances are if I ran him through this personality assessment, he would score high in the Architect category. Still, he needed to attend school and go through years of training to become the competent worker he is today.

Every week I receive dozens of resumés from people wanting to join my team. Not once have I ever made a hire just because someone had a strong profile. I take everything into account such as background, profile, and life experiences. For me, a job interview is not an IQ test.

Sometimes people who interview the worst turn out to be the best fit. Take someone who has an engineer mindset. Most engineers I know have great analytical minds, but they struggle to have strong social skills. They are excellent problem solvers but might not do well in face-to-face meetings. While some interviewers might be tempted to write off such people, I have found they are often the perfect fit if placed in the right position. They aren't going to tear it up on sales, but they might do well at coming up with solutions to complex problems.

As I write this, I think of one of our team members who is rather dry, socially quiet, and tends to take in and listen more than he shares. Several years ago, I brought him in for an interview but did not hire him because I was not sure how he would mesh with others in our group. Still, I saw how he measured up in the personality assessment. He was a Tech Expert, the same profile as another guy in a similar position who was doing very well. And so, sticking with the data and going against my natural impulses, I added him to our team. To my mild surprise, he did very well, even becoming the head of his entire department.

When it comes right down to it, I want people to interview well. But I would rather have someone on my team who interviewed poorly and excelled in their position than I would someone who crushes it in the interview phase but struggles in their new role.

As is often the case, personal referrals tend to produce the highest-quality candidates. When I contact a referral, one of the questions I always ask is, "Would you consider this person to be in the top 10% of people you have worked with in your organization?" If the answer is yes, it's a good chance I have a winner on my hands.

Also, keep in mind that sometimes you might have what you think is the perfect profile created for your job, only to discover someone with a slightly different profile might be the person you need. I remember this one time we were certain that the right profile for the Account Manager position was a Coordinator. But after going through several coordinators in this role, we realized we had made a miscalculation and needed someone with a different profile.

Ultimately, these personality profiles extend to people from various cultural backgrounds, genders, and ethnicities. My philosophy is that I don't care if you are a baby boomer or millennial. If you have the character and competency to be a strong member of our team, I want you on board!

WHERE SHOULD I START?

When it comes to getting the right people in the right seats on the bus, I have discovered many companies fly by the seat of their pants. The results of this way of hiring are destructive and as my friend Mark Connelly notes, "70% of the American workforce is disengaged in their job because they are in the wrong seat on the bus."[33]

A thought I have borrowed from Netflix CEO Reed Hastings is this whole concept of talent density. The idea is

---

33   https://www.weforum.org/agenda/2016/11/70-of-employees-say-they-are-disengaged-at-work-heres-how-to-motivate-them/

that when you work with a bunch of people who are highly talented, everyone's game is elevated.

Sometimes, I think we fear removing people from our team who aren't pulling their weight. We think if we do so, we will slow down our team's progress because we will have less hands-on-deck. But just the opposite is true. When the wrong people are moved off the bus, the remaining people can flourish and take their game to another level – propelling your company to a height it would not reach with the wrong people on board.

One of the main reasons you want the right people on your team is so you can take your organization to a place it can run without you. If you are the thread that holds your company together, you are much less appealing to potential buyers who might want to purchase your company. Individuals and corporations who purchase companies want to see businesses that are self-sustaining and are not run by one leader.

Taking this step of letting go might require you to swallow some ego and recognize that you cannot do everything on your own. In my case, when I first started Vantage, I wanted to prove to my team that no position was beneath me, and I did every task imaginable. Some of this was good and modeled a strong work ethic for our team. However, as we started to grow, I realized I needed to make a change and let go of some of those things I thought only I could do.

At the end of the day, it is a numbers game. You might gulp at the thought of bringing on board someone who will cost you $80,000 a year. But again, if this same person can bring in over twenty properties and cover the entire cost of their salary in year one, this hire is a huge win because the inventory they bring into your business in one year will continue to pay residual income for years to come!

One of the points I rarely hear discussed is the cost of missed opportunity, or opportunity cost. For example, if you have more natural leads coming in than you can feasibly handle, you might end up losing tens of thousands of dollars than if you had hired someone to manage those leads effectively.

Having the right people on your team can make all the difference, so get the wrong people off the bus, the right people on, and sitting in their proper seats!

7

IT ALL STARTS WITH
DATA

CHAPTER SEVEN

It All Starts with Data

"IN GOD WE TRUST. ALL OTHERS, BRING DATA."

— W.E. Deming

The key to great marketing is great data. You can have the best-looking postcards around but if you are hitting the wrong targets, all your time and efforts will produce little fruit.

One of the first steps Vintory takes with every client is to walk them through the basics of developing a strong data list. We have found it is absolutely critical to their success as a company.

Without a solid data file, it does not matter how good your marketing campaigns are. That is why we spend a significant amount of time in the setup phase compiling lists from multiple sources, merging, and appending to get such information as emails and phones, and then segmenting the data we have collected into lists. We want to make sure our clients send the right messages to the right targets at the right time.

Where to Get Your Data?   vintory

Tax Records / MLS   List Brokers   VR Permit Data   Scraped Data

WHERE YOU GET THE DATA

If you are not hitting the right targets, you are sending your marketing dollars down the drain. From my perspective, data is one of the most underestimated tools for inventory acquisition.

I heard a stat one time that 50% of all marketing comes down to the list.[32] This is the reason why Vintory has five data analysts on our team solely focused on getting the right targets for our partners. That's how big of a deal this is. Data allows you to grow smarter and is the most cost effective and time efficient way to grow your inventory.

The first source of data is public tax records. If you are in a state where this information is made available, this is often the best and cheapest method at your disposal. It is often affiliated with MLS services. Some states are a bit of a pain and only allow you to download one record at a time, thus making this process time consuming and cost

---

32 Source

prohibitive.

At this point, you are better off going directly to a list broker. Here you will have to pay for the data. There are hundreds of brokers available. All you need to do is search Google and find one that best meets your needs. Two I recommend are Info USA and Exact Data. These sites are great and have data on just about every single market available. Note: If you decide to go with a list broker, you need to make sure you get both the email and phone number in your contact base. This will make sense later.

The gold nuggets in this database are the information on absentee owner data. This is where the property address and the mailing address of an owner are different. Usually this indicates this property is either their second home or they are a real estate investor.

Another great source of information is vacation rental permit data. In many markets, if you are required to have a permit, you can request a list and the city or town representative is required to make this available. Initially, they might push back and make you jump through a few extra hoops, but just insist they release it due to the Freedom of Information Act. Again, many times they do not make this easy and make you drive down to the courthouse, pay them in person, and download the files onto a jump drive. The key is to be persistent because the data gleaned from this source can be excellent.

If you really want to step up your game, you can even hire someone to scrape data from Online Travel Agencies (OTA's) or your competitors' websites. When this whole process is complete, you have an incredible list of targets at your disposal!

MERGE THE DATA YOU HAVE COLLECTED

Even if you are not a data junkie like me, watching this list come together is a beautiful thing because it signals the start of a strong foundation.

Keep in mind that after you compile these various lists, you will likely need to hire someone who has the skills necessary to take all this data and place it into a single Excel spreadsheet. It will take some time and a little bit of effort, but the benefits that come with having this list far outweigh any negatives.

At Vintory, we have several data analysts who merge and deduplicate all this data into one clean data file. If you do not have someone on your staff who has the time or skillset to take on this responsibility, I recommend visiting an online site such as Upwork or Fiverr and hiring someone who can.

SEGMENT YOUR CONTACTS

Next, it is time to segment the leads you have generated. There are several ways you can do this.

The first is by segmenting your list based on your ideal customer profile (ICP). You then segment your ICP by A, B, and C targets. A target might be based on the income you could generate from a potential property, or they might be those pieces of inventory that fall into your specific niche. I recommend that you reach out to your A targets every month. B targets should be hit on a quarterly basis and C targets once or twice a year.

Another way to segment your list is through the way you send out your marketing campaigns. For example, you might run direct mail, email, custom audiences, and IP targeting to your monthly targets. Then for your B targets you might only do direct mail, email, and custom audiences. For your C targets, maybe you scale back to only direct mail and email. It's up to you how you break this down, but the key is to prioritize those individuals who show the greatest promise of delivering you a return.

A final additional way to segment your list is by persona. This is important because different personas have different pain points. When you know what your potential property owners care about, you can change up your messaging to reach people in a way that connects with them. While this approach might prove to be more labor and time intensive upfront, this is often the most effective way to add new inventory to your portfolio.

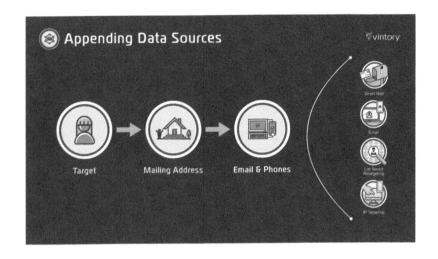

APPEND YOUR DATA SOURCES

Appending means adding additional contact methods to each target record. You can append by adding mailing addresses, emails, or cell phones. This is important because now you can market with an omnichannel marketing approach versus just sending out one or two postcards per year.

This means you can reach people through direct mail, email, and list-based retargeting on various social channels such as Facebook, Instagram, and LinkedIn. The only way you can do this is by appending those data sources.

Usually, your list broker has the ability to do this; but if they can't, they should be able to recommend some different services that can.

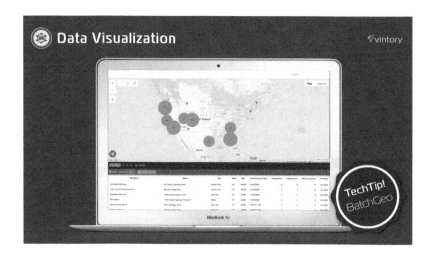

VISUALIZE YOUR DATA

A final step I always recommend for vacation rental managers is that they leverage tools such as BatchGeo or Google My Maps. Through these programs they can see their targets on a map rather than just on a spreadsheet. This is such an underused tool and is important because it allows you to see outliers or anomalies.

You might compile these points on the map based on the potential properties you have or you might do it according to the mailing addresses you have on file. It's up to you. The key is to keep your eyes open.

If you see that a vast majority of your potential customers live in one area, this will help you know how to use your pay per click campaigns so you can leverage them by listing those specific areas.

I think of one vacation rental manager I know who found out there was a town in Ohio that was a hot spot of activity. Even though this town was several hundred miles away from their central hub, he ended up doing some target marketing in this community, flying up, and doing a whole info session for any vacation rental homeowners who had interest. The net result that evening was him landing several new pieces of inventory!

This all happened because he visualized the data he had available, and paid attention to the trends he saw.

DON'T SKIP THE DATA STEP

Never forget that the foundation of all good inventory acquisition starts with data. Without a solid data file, it does not matter how good your marketing efforts are. If you are not hitting the right targets, you are not being effective.

With a solid data file that is merged, and correctly appended, your marketing efforts will become that much more productive. For those of you that find data boring, I challenge you not to skip this step in the process. It is an absolute must.

Yes, it does require some effort and a bit of patience but when you have this step in place, you set yourself up for success.

8

SEVEN STEPS
TO CREATING
EFFECTIVE
MESSAGING

CHAPTER EIGHT

Seven Steps to Creating Effective Messaging

Many organizations tend to stick with a basic approach to marketing that focuses exclusively on features and benefits.

At Vintory, we believe in what is called outcome-based marketing. The goal of outcome-based marketing in the vacation rental space is to focus on the best possible outcome for each property owner. This looks different for each person and is directly tied to their individual pain and pleasure points. For instance, if I coach a client and we both know that many of the homeowners in their region have been burned by listing their home with another vacation rental company that has not treated them well, this will shift our messaging. The outcome will focus less on profit and more on working with a trusted expert.

Money alone is no longer the greatest motivator for these property owners if their homes are not being taken care of in the process. So, instead of saying something like, "List with us and we promise to give you a better rate of return," we might say something like, "Take the headache out of owning a second home." With this shift in verbiage, we move away from the obvious payoff – money – and get to the real reason a homeowner might want to list their home with one of our clients.

Outcome-based marketing is all about honing in on the unique pain and pleasure points each customer has, and tailoring the message to meet their needs. For some homeowners, they do not have the bandwidth to manage a second home and so the pitch to them is, "Go with us and we will limit your stress." Others just want to recoup the expenses they have in owning a second home, and some only care about making as much cash as possible.

At Vintory, we help each one of our partners build out a comprehensive messaging report. This step is critical, because it eliminates much of the guesswork. You're not just sending out postcards and hoping something sticks – known as "spray and pray" marketing. You have a plan tailored to each unique audience you want to partner with.

Any business owner can have dreams and aspirations for their business. The key to rooting these dreams in reality is recognizing the learning curve involved. Great messaging is a science that takes a lot of observation and experimentation. It requires a level of expertise, knowledge, and experience to do an exceptional job and get exceptional results.

To do messaging well, you need to take a step back and gain a 30,000-foot perspective. Ask yourself, what do you want to achieve? Know your audience and identify their likes and dislikes. Only then can you craft a message that motivates your prospects to actions.

It is critical your message connects with people because we live in a world of skim readers. Sure, there are those people who read every word of every page, but most are on their phones, scrolling through social media when they come across your site. It's your goal with messaging to have them slow down, stop, and look at what you have.

And as they stop, you must offer them something valuable that is worth their time. Like writing a book, the marketing process is taking your reader through a journey that motivates them to action.

To do this, there are seven critical components involved.

1. Identify Your Unique Selling Proposition

What is the one thing that sets your business apart? What makes your business better than the competition? How would you summarize this in one sentence?

An organization's unique selling proposition (USP) is sometimes tough to flush out. It is different from a mission or vision statement and is the key to determining success in the marketplace.

To be blunt, many organizations are rather vanilla in their approach to crafting a strong USP. They resort to trite phrases such as, "Go with us and you will make money," but do not realize their messaging is no different than 90% of their competition.

When I first started Vantage, this was not something I did well. In the back of my mind, I had an idea of how we were different from the competition. We were providing a four-star experience that was comparable to a hotel whereas our competitors weren't even providing bedsheets. But the thoughts in my head did not translate into the messaging we sent out.

Now, this step is one of the first things I encourage new clients to nail down. Sometimes this process takes days to figure out as I help clients study the marketplace and determine their fit. At Vintory, it's easy because we are the only sales and marketing platform for the vacation rental space dedicated to growing inventory. But with most other companies they are one of many, and must create messaging that sets them apart.

Take for example the shoe company Toms. For years they ran a basic campaign, "Buy one, give one." The messaging was clear. Buy one shoe, and we will give another shoe to someone in need. To date, they have impacted over 100,000,000 people with this message. It's powerful, it's simple, and it connects so much better than if they had just stuck a sign on the door that said, "We have great shoes!"

Another example is a partner of ours named Terry. When we first started drilling down into the data on his company, we realized he was crushing it. From the empirical data we saw, Terry was miles ahead of competitors in his region. His ability to market properties was unparalleled and we understood this was his USP. He could provide customers a solid rate of return because he was so great at his job!

In a world of similarity, you need something to make you stand out. So, ask yourself, what is that one thing that sets me apart from my competition? Then write and rewrite this distinction until you can state and market it in a single sentence.

2. List Your Features and Benefits

This takes us to the core of this chapter. Features and benefits are the key factors that make your company special. Features are factual statements and benefits are how these features help people.

In Michael Masterson's book *Ready, Fire, Aim: Zero to $100 Million in No Time Flat*, he shares the story of Schlitz beer. Founded in 1849, this company became one of ten brewing companies in the U.S. As Masterson noted, "All of them—including Schlitz—emphasized the same basic benefit: Our beer is pure. To try to separate themselves from the pack, Schlitz hired a marketing consultant who began by taking a tour of their facility and asking dozens and dozens of questions. He was impressed with what he heard: that the company had conducted 1,623 experiments over five years to identify the finest mother yeast cell that could produce the richest taste and flavor; that the water was distilled by being heated to 5,000 degrees before it was used to brew beer; that the bottles were sterilized at 1,600 degrees; and that every batch of beer was tested for quality before it was shipped out. The painstaking brewing and bottling processes fascinated the consultant. He told Schlitz management that they should describe the steps they take to assure purity to their customers. 'But all brewing companies do the same thing,' the managers said.[32]

"But no one in your industry has ever told their customers how they do it," the consultant persisted. "If you get the word out first, you will gain distinction and prominence in the marketplace, even if you don't really deserve it."

32   Masterson, Michael. Ready, Fire, Aim: Zero to $100 Million in No Time Flat. Hoboken, NJ: John Wiley, 2008. 102.

"Through their USP, Schlitz made the word pure take on a very different and much more tangible meaning to all beer drinkers around the country," executive coach Jay Abraham explained. "Schlitz began using this preemptive marketing USP, and within six months Schlitz beer moved from number eight in market sales to number one."[33]

This story underscores the importance of featuring the benefits you have to offer. Like Schlitz, it might be as simple as emphasizing the meticulous cleaning process you offer. During my time with Vantage, between every guest's stay, we had a professional cleaning company come and give the entire house a cleaning. Then, we had a supervisor inspect. And then another person white glove the place to make sure it looked great. We treated this role seriously and made sure our customers and homeowners knew the steps we took.

Because when you think about it, you aren't selling housekeeping. That's just a feature. You're selling the joy of owning a vacation home without the stress and backaches of cleaning it yourself. You're selling the ability to give guests a memorable first impression when they walk into your clean home and relax after a long trip. You're selling that both your guests and homeowners can trust that they are staying in a clean and hygienic place.

So when you separate features from benefits, you separate what "is" from what "does." In turn, you can speak more directly to your ideal homeowner, and show them the life they can expect to have with you as their property manager.

---

33   Jay Abraham, Getting Everything You Can Out of All You've Got (New York: Truman Talley Books/St. Martin's Griffin, 2001). 81-84.

3. Social Proof Your Image

After the key features and benefits have been outlined, it's time to use social proof. All this means is that you highlight other people who have signed up for your service and found it useful. In short, let the five-star reviews speak for themselves.

When you're surfing the web and you see a testimonial from an industry expert, that's social proof. When you are viewing a pricing page and you see that a well-respected company is using that product, that's social proof. Essentially, it's borrowing third-party influence to sway potential customers.

Of course, this will be different depending on what kind of proof you have. It might be featuring video testimonials or one paragraph endorsements from clients who have been positively impacted by your company. Then, as you grow, you learn to tailor these testimonials to target specific homeowners who find these endorsements useful. For example, when you send out marketing material to a specific community, it is a great idea to have another homeowner from that community featured in your promotion. This strengthens people's trust in your message.

On your website, you can create site landing pages that are geared to specific communities. Always keep in mind that you want to use references from people that are close to the targets you are going after. If you know one of your clients is an attorney, send them promotional material with an attorney featured in the content. Essentially, you are doing your best to solve any objections a prospective owner might have.

Then, as you sign people up, spread the love on social media and make these announcements on your page. When other companies see this, they will take note and you will gain more trust in your industry and generate more word-of-mouth referrals.

4. Spotlight Your Trust Icons

Speaking of trust, this brings us to Trust Icons. Along with referrals, achievements such as an A+ rating with the Better Business Bureau (BBB) provide an additional level of credibility. If you are an Airbnb Superhost, have a great Google or Facebook rating, or have other local credentials with the local Chamber of Commerce, these need to be featured on your site.

I don't know about you, but whenever I visit a new site, it helps if I see Trust Icons, such as 4.8 stars with Trustpilot. This sets my mind at ease and helps me see others trust this company.

If you do not have any of these Trust Icons on your site, work at getting some. Get involved in your community and earn some badges that add to your credibility.

5. Create a Compelling Offer

Next, develop a compelling offer and feature it on all your messaging. Keep in mind that while 50% of your success is based on your list, at least 30% of your success is creating an enticing compelling offer.

A compelling offer is also known as an "irresistible offer" or a "mafia offer." It's called "mafia offer" from the movie *The Godfather* where Marlon Brando playing Don Corleone said, "I'm gonna make him an offer he can't refuse."

What makes up the best compelling offers? First, they offer great value. They deliver a discount and a premium. They also very often include bonuses. Who doesn't love a great bonus?

Second, the benefit needs to be relevant to the intended audience. For example, an offer for free dog food isn't relevant to a person who doesn't own a pet.

Next, they have a sense of urgency and require an immediate response. For example, "Call before March 31st to receive your FREE Smart Home package." The urgency can also come from a potential loss due to inaction. People nearly always prioritize not losing something over getting more of something.

And lastly, they include a strong risk reversal (more to come on that next section).

Another thing to consider is what is the offer in exchange for (and how quickly can they collect on the offer). Successful marketing requires getting your target customer to jump over a series of increasingly higher hurdles (requests).

To get someone over a hurdle, the reward on the other side of the hurdle needs to greatly outweigh the cost or effort required to get over the hurdle. A truly irresistible offer is lopsided in the customer's favor.

When you're sending a piece of marketing communication, you should always have a goal in mind, and you should make it extremely clear to the prospect exactly what it is you want them to do.

Most of the time, the goal is going to be a click, an email reply, a phone call or a form submission. Later in the cycle, an ask might be setting up a meeting or signing a management agreement. So, you need to make it clear that you want them to click through to this web page, you want them to call you, or you want them to reply to the email you sent them, fill out a form, book a meeting, buy something, etc.

Then, you need to make it clear what they get for doing that, and when they get it. People love instant gratification, so a reward they get right away is better than a reward they get at a later time or after jumping over one or more additional hurdles. If you're giving them a long-term offer (meaning one down the sales cycle), it needs to be that much bigger.

You can also throw in additional offers in exchange for later hurdles. In fact, you can even mix short-term offers with long-term offers in your messages. For example, get a $50 gift card for booking a meeting and get 30% off if you sign up by the end of the month. If people can see strong benefits in the path ahead and minimal risk and effort, they're more likely to walk down that path.

Finally, the offer has to be realistic. The prospect can't think it is too good to be true, or they'll just ignore it. In order to prove the offer is real, sometimes you need to add a "because" to the offer.

Let's use some examples from Gary Bencivenga (perhaps the most successful copywriter of all time):

- We're having a "fire sale" where everything in the store is 75% off. Why? Because we just had a fire in our store and clothes smell like a campfire.

- Or, we're having a "walk-in" special where everything is 50% off, because they're doing construction in front of the shop, so you're going to have to park further away because people can't park that close.

Studies have shown that pretty much any "because" is effective. In fact, the famous study I'm referring to was one where someone was using a copy machine and another person approaches and asks them if they can skip ahead and use the copy machine. When the approaching person didn't give a reason, their success rate went way down. But, if they gave a reason, even a "because I need to use it" the success rates went up dramatically.

You can also offer social proof around your offer. If it's a free giveaway, throw in a quote from someone similar to the prospect talking about how valuable it was to them. You could also show how many similar people have claimed the offer. Your proof can be anything that proves that what is on the other side of the hurdle is real, valuable, and worth the effort.

My acid test for a good compelling offer is to assume a potential customer is standing over the trashcan going through the mail and dropping piece after piece of junk mail into the trash. When they get to your postcard and they read your compelling offer, does it cause them to pause for a couple seconds and put it on the counter for another look? If so, that's a great compelling offer and that's the point.

So, to recap. A good compelling offer needs to have the following elements:

- Has great value
- Is relevant to the prospect
- Increases urgency

- Leverages risk reversals
- Is lopsided in favor of the prospect
- Offers instant gratification (if possible)
- Has a clear "ask" (what they need to do to claim it)
- Is believable

6. Provide a Strong Risk Reversal

Along with a compelling offer, you should feature a guarantee that takes away the fear of signing up. This is called a Risk Reversal. A Risk Reversal is a strategy that transfers some (or all) of the risk of a transaction from the buyer to the seller. Examples of risk reversals include "No Start-up Fees" or "No Long-Term Contracts" or "Risk-Free Guarantee" where you can cancel and get a refund of your rental management fees. These Risk Reversals reduce friction in the buying process.

When businesses have a high startup fee and long-term commitments baked into the signup process, it's tough to get people to buy in. The ask is just too high and the unknown too great.

Instead, start with small asks and baby steps that allow interested parties to become engaged, all without signing their life away.

One of the best examples of a risk-reversal was from Evolve Vacation Rentals. Their "Risk Free Guarantee" allows homeowners to cancel their management contract at six months and get a full refund of management fees. This is an absolutely brilliant strategy and will definitely increase their conversions. The small percentage of people that take them up on this refund will be offset by the large increased number of new homeowners they landed into their rental program that normally wouldn't have signed up. I highly recommend deploying a strategy like this to all of our partners.

7. Always Present a Call to Action (CTA)

There is no point in doing a marketing piece if there is no CTA. What are you asking prospective owners to do? Should they call, fill out a form, or email you? There's only one way they can know: You have to tell them.

Whatever you do in this step, make it simple. On your website, have a clear button to push. Don't ask too many questions, and get just as much information as you need.

Along with this, it is always a good idea to have multiple CTAs. Increasingly, we have discovered that unlike my parents' generation, younger consumers do not want to talk with people on the phone. So, whenever we send out information, we include both a number to call or text.

As my marketing director Alex points out, there has been a shift in marketing approach in recent years. Traditional marketing thirty years ago featured tons of in-your-face content. Then, content marketing shifted the perspective to adding value to customers. In their efforts to come across as trustworthy, some companies have gone too far and now have little to no calls to action.

In our busy society, people need to be told what to do. If they are scrolling through social media and come across your post, they should know exactly what you want them to do with the material they see. To see this in action, I encourage you to visit www.vintory.com and look for the CTAs we use throughout our homepage. See what I did there? Always give people a clear next step that brings them through your sales funnel.

REMEMBER THE GOAL

Remember, in all these steps you are eliminating barriers and making it easy for new homeowners to sign up. If your goal is to increase your inventory, you need to operate with this in mind.

So, where should you start? The first step I would say you should take is to come up with a cohesive messaging plan that transcends all your marketing channels. At Vintory, we recommend building out a Key Messaging Report that becomes your baseline for all marketing projects. Doing so gets you out of the "hope for the best" mindset and takes you into the world of reality.

I encourage you to use this seven-step process as a blueprint for the way you message. Write these points down on a notecard and stick it on your desk. Then, as you craft messaging with these seven steps in mind, your customers will take notice and your inventory portfolio will expand.

9

CREATE A GREAT
LANDING PAGE AND
TRACK YOUR LEADS

CHAPTER NINE

Create a Great Landing Page and Track Your Leads

All seven of the marketing points we listed in the last chapter should come together with your landing page. Having a strong landing page is one of the most important things you can do to add inventory and it's also the lowest hanging fruit because you have already done the hard work of getting people to come to your site. Your website and your landing page are your brand, it's your image, it's a reflection of you and your company. A potential owner will instantly get a good understanding of your company within seconds by just looking at your website and landing page.

If your page is ambiguous and does not have a clear place where homeowners can go and find out more information, you are missing out on potentially hundreds of leads. Many times, when I visit a vacation rental company website, I cannot find a clear landing page for homeowners. The owner of the company is so concerned with getting more guests that they have lost sight of the real revenue needle-mover, new owners. So instead of having a page that is readily accessible to property owners, they keep it tucked away in some obscure portion of their website and make would-be owners jump through a series of unnecessary hoops to gain more information.

If obtaining more inventory is the most important aspect of your business, it is critical that you have something that points homeowners in the right direction.

START WITH GREAT LOOKING LANDING PAGE

On your landing page, I suggest you start with a compelling "hero image." Don't just take a generic picture from a free site online and slap it on your site. Hire a photographer and capture a high-quality picture that features your company in the best possible light. I would even encourage you to use different photos of your different homes for different landing pages.

When this is done, make sure the other pictures on your site are up to date. Every owner has different tastes. If you run a vacation rental company in Tennessee, you might want a site that is forest green, and highlights the gorgeous landscape. If you are in the Blue Ridge Mountains, a blue theme might be more appropriate. And if you are in a trendier upscale neighborhood, a more minimalist approach might be best. The key is to know your area, and make sure your site reflects the properties you have.

Another basic step is to make sure your font choice and wording is written in such a way that your main message stands out. Include details for people (like my wife) who read every word. But make sure you keep the main points in bold lettering so that skim readers like myself don't click away before giving you a chance.

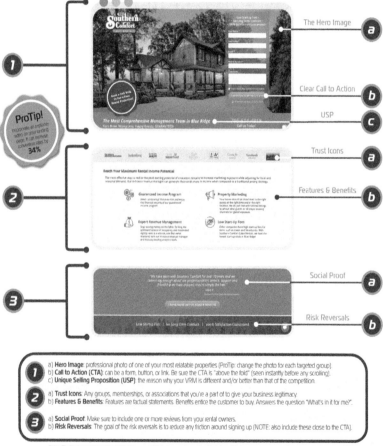

www.vintory.com | 410-401-8010

Regardless of your context, do not skimp on your website design. It might be tempting to save a few bucks and go with a cheap site that you can have up and running by the end of the day, but I would encourage you to be methodical in this step, and talk with someone who can help you design a site that will grow with you, and meet your needs at every size of your business.

INCORPORATE ALL SEVEN MESSAGING STEPS

Now, think back to all of the messaging steps we outlined in the last chapter, and make it a point to intentionally incorporate all seven in your landing page.

Start with your unique selling proposition. This needs to be in a prominent place on the site and should instantly grab the reader's attention. We have a partner who owns Mountain Laurel Chalets and they provide a great example of this.[32] Their business is located in Gatlinburg, Tennessee, and their messaging leaps off the page. The banner that highlights their website says it all: "Maximize your profit, minimize your stress." That is their sales pitch, and their unique angle is peace of mind. Yes, they will offer you a profit, but the main question they pose to homeowners is this: "Is your rental home a frustration or a pleasure?"

Along with your USP needs to be your compelling offer. Don't count on the fact that someone already knows your business before they visited your site. They might have come across your site by chance through a Google search

32   https://www.mtnlaurelchalets.com/maximize-your-profit-minimize-your-stress

and know very little about what you have to offer.

Your features and benefits should likewise be obvious. One of our partners who does a fantastic job with this is Southern Comfort Cabin When they click on this, they find a list of Rentals. When you visit their website, homeowners see a tab at the top of the screen where they can list their home.[33] When they click on this they find a list of all the features and benefits available. Some of these include:

- "Exclusively Focused on Vacation Rentals" This tells you their attention is not divided.

- "Expert In-House Revenue Management" They are going to get you a great return!

- "Direct Booking Strength" 70% of all reservations come through their site directly without going through a third-party service, thus ensuring more money for everyone involved.

- "Powerful Property Marketing" They tailor their listings to attract the right people.

- "Low Start-Up Fees" They have the lowest fees in their region.

- "Multi-Channel Marketing System" Even though they receive 70% of bookings through their site, they have a strong presence in places like VRBO and Airbnb.[34]

Notice how all these features set them apart from other vacation rental companies. It's not that other companies are not doing any of these things, but Southern Comfort does a better job of highlighting what they have to

---

33   Southerncomfortcabinrentals.com
34   https://www.southerncomfortcabinrentals.com/list-your-home.htm

offer. They don't just tell you they are the best. They show you and let you decide. This is how successful vacation rental businesses operate.

Along with listing your features and benefits, social proof your site with great testimonials and include those Trust Icons to give you the credibility you deserve. Don't forget to include at the bottom of your page a solid risk reversal such as: "100% satisfaction guaranteed."

Most importantly, have a clear call to action. Below your quick fill out form, have a highlighted tab people can click to submit their information and get in contact with a member of your team.

MICROSITES

As I was building out Vantage, I stumbled across a strategy that became quite successful for our growth strategy. We built out "micro" websites, known as microsites for each community and building we wanted to gain market share in. We identified the following communities and buildings as high-value targets: Sunset Island, Meridian, Belmont Towers, Gateway Grand, and Rivendell. These were newer communities that rented very well, had high nightly rates, and had a strong repeat following from the guests.

We would build out a microsite for each community and it ended up having great traffic not only from guests, but more importantly, vacation rental homeowners who owned in these communities. Most of these communities didn't have a website, so we became the de facto community website. This plan turned out to be very successful and we attracted many new owners leveraging this strategy.

RECORD AN EXPLAINER VIDEO

In addition to all these steps, it is always a great idea to have an explainer video. If a picture is worth a thousand words, a video might be worth ten thousand. In two-to-three minutes, you can outline your business in a way that might connect more than all the other info pages on your site combined.

You might record a friendly hello and tell more about yourself, or even feature several clients of yours that have been happy with the service you provide. Companies that do explainer videos have found the rewards can be great. For example, one of Salesforce's business units started including videos, and found they increased their conversion rates by 20%!

HAVE A CHAT BOT

Chat bots are another way to increase these conversion rates. Whenever people come on Vintory's site, we have a popup chat bot so a member of our team can engage with them.

Because more and more people like the convenience factor of chat in place of a phone, having a chat widget at the bottom corner of your site can be a great way to connect with new leads. For example, just this morning my wife was looking at a product online. She had some questions about the product but didn't want to phone since it was still early in the morning. Fortunately, this company had a chat bot and she was able to get her questions answered within a few seconds. Several minutes later she made an order! It is unlikely this would have happened if this company did not have chat.

Whenever a new chat conversation starts on our website, I receive a notification. Several times a day, someone from my team (including myself) is answering the questions people have. All of this makes for a much stronger customer experience, and reduces friction in the buyer's journey.

10

USE A CRM TO
TRACK YOUR LEADS

CHAPTER TEN

Use a CRM to Track Your Leads

It is critical you use some form of customer relationship management software or CRM. Post-it notes and legal pads will not suffice. Great CRM software programs include Salesforce, Hubspot, Zoho CRM, and even Vintory. CRM programs can save you a significant amount of time by keeping all your leads in one place. If you don't know where to start, I would recommend Hubspot. Their basic CRM features are free and, even though their add-ons can be pricey, the basic CRM service they provide is everything you will need if you are just starting out.

In my previous company, we signed up for Salesforce. We hired an outside firm and had them set it up including all of the automations. It was incredible, and saved us hundreds of hours and helped us close tons of deals. Unfortunately, the setup was not cheap, and we ended up spending close to $30,000.

Because quality leads are super expensive, and thus super valuable, you need to look at each lead as a potential nugget of gold. Treat them with care and do not allow anything to chance.

LEVERAGE THE POWER OF AUTOMATION

You've heard the saying that the shortest pencil beats the longest memory. The same is true with automation. When you have your CRM in place, there is no excuse for missing a single lead, ever.

Through the power of software, you can drag, drop, and hit play, and these tools will do all the work for you. The best part is that marketing automation will ensure no new lead falls through the cracks. Since it is often the first person who responds to a prospect that gets the deal, automation makes sure you respond to your customers in real time. As soon as a new lead comes in, even if you are in bed, there is a system in place to connect with this new owner and get them the right information.

I like to organize my leads into two buckets – new leads and long-term nurture leads. New leads are those people who are ready to sign up right away. They want information and they want to have a conversation today.

Long-term nurture leads take some time to develop. They might be interested, but either they have never listed their home with a company before, or they are hesitant to get out of the current deal they have with another business. Through automation, you can stay in contact with these long-term leads and send a series of preplanned strategic messages. We've found some of our partners close as much as 50% of their deals that were in their long-term nurture stage.

THE ULTIMATE FORMULA FOR FOSTERING LEADS

Many people think all they need to do is capture the lead, input the lead, and follow up. It's a simple one, two, three step process! But this is seldom the case. Most times there are unforeseen obstacles that arise, looking to kill the deal before it gains any traction.

It's important to build a strong follow up process to convert leads, especially if you feel you're not the most persuasive person.

A salesperson with determination and follow up skills will often outpace a salesperson relying on persuasion alone. Continue to hone both, and you'll be consistently on top. Look out world!

Jade Wolff is one of our business development leaders. She shares the following pieces of advice:

Tip 1: Use a CRM System

My first recommendation is for you to use a great CRM system. Having all your leads up in the cloud, easy to sort and keep track of the sales process for each, will save you endless hours of administrative work so you can get back to the business of selling.

Through utilizing a great CRM, you can track just the kind of information you need. Your goal with each lead is to develop a full profile of the type of person they are. Yes, the basic data such as name, phone number, and email address is helpful, but then you want to know other things such as the number of bedrooms in their house, or their unique pain points.

Whenever a new lead comes in, I always make it a practice to spend 80% of my time listening. In my head, I knew the seven or eight key benefits our company offered. But rather than just blurting all these out, I listened to what mattered most to the customer and then I tailored my delivery to suit their needs.

Working with a CRM is not just inputting leads, it's creating tags and fields for sorting and setting tasks for follow up. It's important to do this in the beginning with each lead because it's too time consuming to go back and do later.

Tip 2: Capture Customer Notes

No detail is too small. One of the most crucial pieces of inputting leads is the notes you take. I cannot stress this enough. Leave meticulous notes, especially the first note from the discovery conversation.

My first notes can be a bit extra. They are long, and contain every bit of info I could gather from my targeted questions, but there are also a lot of miscellaneous details. If they mentioned where they recently went on vacation, I put that down. If we talked about a certain restaurant they like, I'll include that. If their dog barked in the background, I probably asked about it and got its name and breed. Again, I wrote that down. Why? Because the details can be good ice breakers in the future and help me remember who this person is, besides the fact that they have a nice property.

Tip 3: Build a Comprehensive Lead Summary

Remembering things in threes is one of my quirks, and you are welcome to adopt it. I want to know about a lead's past, present, and future. Have they rented the home before? Why and why not? What are they doing with the home now? What do they want to do with it in the future?

A summary of that might look like this: *Never rented before, never had a desire to, currently doing some upgrades to the kitchen, retiring in the near future and need the extra money.*

Notes are especially useful and important when more than one person is on a sales team, or a manager will need to see how things are going and what the sales pipeline looks like. If your lead calls while you are not available or even on vacation your teammates can read your notes and be up to speed quickly and save both the lead and themselves time and confusion.

Tip 4: Plan Out Your Next Steps Ahead of Time, Make an Appointment, and Close!

It's important to have next steps worked out. Once you have a lead, you'll need to convert it, and the best way to do that, besides follow up, is creating a pipeline of next steps. A sales pipeline needs to move forward as swiftly as possible, and it's up to you to apply the water pressure with your actions.

Capture the lead, input the lead, and follow up. Easy as 1, 2, 3, right? Well, if you are waiting for someone to "get back to you," you'll be waiting forever. So, propose next steps with a property walkthrough appointment or an income projection appointment. Don't just email the income projection because that's where most ghosting happens. Make an appointment to go over the details together and then find out what their objections are to signing up and address them. If it's a walkthrough, bring the contract and start explaining it at the end of the tour, and go for the close.

Tip 5: Be Assertive!

Remember that if you are not assertive, other agents will be and you're up against them. Feel the lead out and go as far as you can with them without turning them off. It's a skill that takes practice. Build rapport by finding common ground, and it will help to earn their trust and win them over.

Call first and set aside time for accelerating your sales pipeline. If a lead says they'll "call you back," give them a call anyway. People are busy and you can save them time by calling first. Generally, people don't mind if you use a pleasant tone and say you know how busy they are and want to spare them the task.

When I do follow up, I make a task for myself in the CRM. If I really want to be sure to call them at a specific time, I put it on my calendar. And I put an hour or two block on my calendar on Tuesdays, Wednesdays, and Thursdays, as these are proven to be the best days of week to reach people. Then I stick to it!

Tip 6: Work Quickly!

Alternate between calls, texts, and emails. If you call and leave a message one day, email or text the next. Do it in the CRM so you can keep track of the exact time you reached out; that way, the next time you reach out you can try a different time of day. Don't let more than a few days go by when working a lead. Time kills all deals, and the person might be shopping around or sidetracked by other projects.

Tip 7: My Secret for Long Term Leads

Long term nurture is necessary for some leads. If a lead is doing renovations, is a buyer, or has some other situation, you will want to be careful that you don't bug them too much. Instead, make a regular habit to browse recent articles relevant to owners of vacation homes and send them those articles with a quick note: "Thought you might like this article," and you'll be top of mind when they are ready.

Tip 8: Remember that Drip Campaigns = Efficiency!

A CRM that has plenty of automation will be a great way to stay ahead of follow up and minimize the time you spend on it. A drip campaign that has the articles loaded already and is set to trickle out at a set time is a great asset. You can simply drop leads into the campaign (or others!) you created and get back to the business of selling.

11

A BETTER
APPROACH TO
MARKETING

CHAPTER ELEVEN

A Better Approach to Marketing

"STARTING AND BEING CONSISTENT AND NOT GIVING UP IS MORE IMPORTANT THAN BEING BRILLIANT."

– Mark Schaefer

The next several chapters cover the importance of marketing. But before we enter these, it is critical I point out the importance of maintaining an active marketing plan.

When it comes to marketing your vacation rental management company, the competition is red hot! From national agencies to your local family-run shop, everyone is trying to capture the attention of homeowners. As of 2020, there are 23,000 vacation rental companies in the U.S. alone![32] Each one of them would love nothing more than to snatch away your prospects and get your owners to jump ship.

---

32   https://ipropertymanagement.com/research/vacation-rental-industry-statistics

For vacation rental management companies, being proactive and marketing all year is essential to maintaining an edge over the competition.

IS HOMEOWNER MARKETING IN LOW SEASON EFFECTIVE?

Every vacation rental management business has a limited amount of money they devote to marketing. There is no margin to throw away money and not receive a great return on investment.

Some VRMs think they can save themselves a few bucks by cutting back their marketing budget during low seasons, but this is a grave mistake. If you do this, you are giving your competitors the perfect opportunity to step in and get in front of your properties and potential prospects. By the time your owners are waving goodbye, any marketing effort you attempt to retain them will not be enough.

You might think spending your marketing dollars during the off-season or when owners aren't shopping for VRMs is a fruitless effort, but that could not be further from the truth.

Gaining the trust of an owner takes time. You do not convince owners to make a switch to your company overnight. In fact, the first interaction with your brand to a signed contract often takes months, if not years. Perhaps you have heard of the secret rule of seven that says your prospective buyers will need to see or hear your marketing message at least seven times before they will buy your product or service.[33] I have found this to be accurate.

The key to not only converting a lead, but also retaining that customer, is building a relationship and establishing trust. Marketing is not a one and done approach. One study from a customer engagement company SDL found it takes two years for brands to build trust with clients.[34]

Not every part of your budget will generate an immediate return. However, carving aside a portion of your marketing budget specifically for keeping your brand at the forefront of prospects' minds during the low season will have a long-term positive impact on your bottom line. Consistency is key to building a big picture successful homeowner acquisition marketing plan.

There is a reason why car dealerships, insurance companies, and lawyers are ruthless with consistent advertising. Why? Because there is power in developing memorable moments over long periods of time that trigger people to act when the time is right.

VRMs that use off-time marketing come out way ahead of their competition. As competition gets tougher and many mergers and acquisitions take place in the market, acquiring new properties will become more difficult. This only increases the importance of establishing your brand and keeping "top of mind" awareness.

---

33 https://www.brafton.com/blog/content-marketing/marketing-rule-of-7/
34   https://www.entrepreneur.com/article/237579

COLLECT LEADS AND DATE *ALL* YEAR LONG

Brick and mortar stores see spikes during the holiday season. Does this mean they close their doors and stop marketing for the rest of the year? Of course not.

Continuing to market your vacation rental management company throughout the year allows you to continuously grow your list of leads and accumulate more data about your prospects. This data and these new leads will be invaluable when the high season rolls around, and you can start pushing out more targeted and sales-driven campaigns.

Remember that the marketing cost for acquiring a new owner is exponentially higher than the cost of retaining the ones that you have. According to Outbound Engine, acquiring a new client can cost five times as much in comparison to retaining an existing client. In addition, increasing customer retention by 5% can increase profits from 25-95%![35]

Marketing in the off-season and keeping in touch with your owners will keep you at the forefront of their minds. It is important to remind them why they signed up for your vacation rental management services. People have short attention spans, and not continuing contact with owners year-round will make your competitors' offer more compelling.

---

35   https://www.outboundengine.com/blog/customer-retention-marketing-vs-customer-acquisition-marketing/#:~:text=Acquiring%20a%20new%20customer%20can,customer%20is%205%2D20%25.

USE OPTIMAL MESSAGING IN YOUR HOMEOWNER MARKETING

Again, common complaints VRMs have about running year-long campaigns is running out of ideas and wasting marketing dollars.

Both can be resolved if you look at the data. By running seasonal campaigns for low and high seasons, you will find it easier to generate ideas. You can get more specific in your messaging, and these more targeted messages will have a greater impact.

The campaigns you run during the low season don't necessarily need the budget of high season campaigns. There are plenty of budget marketing ideas out there. Email drip campaigns with plain text email are simple to execute and require no design or production budget.

One idea might be to gear your messaging toward sharing your services and benefits. Your goal might not be to get them to make an immediate switch, but you are being present in their lives and on that day they look to make a change, you are at the forefront of their minds.

Effective marketing is critical to your success.

12

OMNICHANNEL
MARKETING PLAN

CHAPTER TWELVE

Omnichannel Marketing Plan

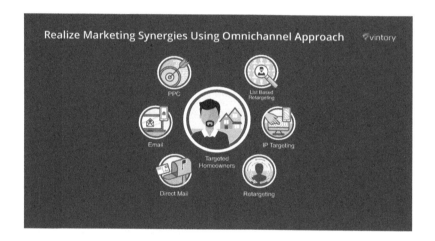

The whole concept of omnichannel marketing is just a fancy term for making sure all your marketing efforts work together to achieve a desired result. It is the definition of synergy. By getting all your marketing channels on the same page, you are creating a symbiotic relationship and maximizing your efforts.

By combining all these strategies, a compounding effect takes place. It goes well beyond those old days of sending out one or two postcards a year. Through your combined efforts, you are putting constant pressure on the market. It's what the big companies like McDonalds do all the time.

Essentially, you are building on the previous chapters. You know your numbers, have created a plan, and have this great treasure trove of data at your fingertips. Now that you have these foundational pillars in place, you can market effectively to the people who want to hear your message.

DIRECT MAIL MARKETING

The first way you can do this is through direct mail. For some industries, direct mail has gone the way of the dodo bird. However, in the vacation rental market, it is one of the most effective ways to connect with a new property owner. It has a compounding effect and the ROI is great.

On average, direct mail is kept in a household for seventeen days. This is useful for your business as it not only gives you access to the recipient, but their network as well. When a potential lead comes over to your recipient's home and the topic of vacation rentals comes up, they will have your well-designed postcard to pull out.

The problem for many rookie marketers is almost always one of three things. For starters, they do not do it consistently! Maybe they send out one or two mail campaigns, grow discouraged with the results, and stop. They assume it doesn't work and fail to develop a big picture perspective. If given the choice between two options, I would rather send a thousand postcards six times to the same targets than I would six thousand postcards once to six thousand different individuals. Consistency is key. I'll say it again... consistency is key.

When I was with Vantage, we saw people respond a year or two after they received one of our cards. Often, when people first receive a card, they are not ready to list their property or switch from their current vacation rental company. If you stick with it and continue to remain present in their lives, they will remember you at the right time. It might be in October when the season has ended, and they discover their home was poorly managed. It might be at a random season when a job situation makes listing their home a necessity.

Another reason rookie direct mail markets struggle is their offer is not compelling. It does not grab their reader's attention and so their mail ends up going in the trash. Along with this, their mail is always the same bland postcard no one wants to read. Every card is the same.

The key with direct mail is to get noticed. Remember that there is that three-second window every mail piece receives where the recipient determines whether your advertisement will be set aside for consideration, or tossed in a trash bin.

Here are five steps we have found helpful that will ensure your direct mail remains on their counter.

Step 1: Develop a Catchy Headline

Your headline should be short and snappy, immediately grabbing the attention of your audience. Two examples of great headlines include:

- *More Money, Less Stress: Start Renting Your Vacation Home!*

- *Relax and Let Us Handle It: We Take Care of Marketing and Maintaining Your Home!*

This step is all about connecting with the pain points of your audience. Notice what the two above examples do. They target those owners who have a vacation property they want on the market. Unfortunately, the time and stress of trying to rent it out have prevented them from doing so. This is where companies like yours can help.

Step 2: Only Use Beautiful Imagery

The photos you chose for your postcards will convey as much, if not more information than the copy. When choosing imagery, you need to make sure you select high-quality images.

If it is a photo, it needs to be of a professional standard. While stock images can often be the budget-friendly way to go, using your own images is the better route to go. You don't want your postcard compared with a competitor that used the same image.

Step 3: Create Stand-Out Colors

Keep in mind that three-second rule we touched on earlier. Your property owner is holding your card just inches above the trashcan along with a stack of mail from other advertisers. You have one shot to get their attention and so you need to make your postcard stand out. Use colors that are eye-catching and will attract interest.

However, it is also worth noting you should not jump too far from your branding. You need to keep the postcard recognizable to your brand and should pick colors that are in-line with your brand guidelines.

Step 4: Highlight a Compelling Offer

I cannot continue to emphasize this enough. Compelling

offers are what will get your phones to ring! This means you must go beyond simply listing or describing the features of your services and offer your recipient something that is impossible to refuse.

Some examples of compelling offers are:

- *Guaranteed Rental Income*
- *Guaranteed to Make You More Money*
- *Receive a Free Smart Home Package*
- *Receive Discounted Commission for the 1st Year*

View your compelling offer as a hook – something that would be hard to ignore. Use as few words as possible and increase the font size of your compelling offer so that your recipient can't miss what you must share.

The best compelling offers offer great value, they deliver a discount or premium, they require immediate response, they include a strong call to action, they have a bulletproof guarantee, and they include risk reversals.

Step 5: Include Your Contact Information

This step seems obvious but make sure you include multiple ways for the recipient to contact you. Phone, text, email, QR Codes, or landing pages. If you have a specific offer you are marketing you may use a more specific number or email for them to contact. If it is a more general postcard, you may simply wish to give your main reception phone number and email. Then, double and triple check to make sure this information is accurate. I've burned many direct mail pieces by having transposed a phone number.

Step 6: Have a Clear Call to Action

Tell your audience what you want them to do. This step should be connected to your compelling offer and motivate people to act on what they see.

Additional Steps

Remember, consistency is key to building a long-term successful homeowner acquisition marketing plan. There's a reason car dealerships, insurance companies, and lawyers are ruthless with consistent advertising.

These industries would miss out on most new business opportunities if they were inconsistent with marketing. Would the Geico Gecko be remembered if he only appeared once a year in a commercial? Of course not. We can all agree this would not be a strong strategy for sustainable success, but this is like what some property management companies expect from their inconsistent marketing strategies.

Along with consistency, vary up your approach. When I was with Vantage, we sent a variety of pieces to property owners. The first was a catchy postcard that established our brand. Weeks later this would be followed up with a "handwritten note." I put this in quotation marks because I learned that even though handwritten messages received a much greater return, they were very time consuming. Now, I use robots and our system is so good that many of these go out automatically without my knowledge. The more customized your card is, the better it will be received. Since we have started customization, we have noticed a 500% increase in return.

After we send a handwritten note, we often send a

market report for their area followed by a flyer that helps them get to know our company. If there is an area of homes we know will promise a high return, we even send in a photographer to take pictures of each home and then send out customized pieces of literature with their home on the front. This is powerful!

The key is to be consistent, strategic, and get people's attention.

EMAIL MARKETING

Along with direct mail, a person's email is one of the most valuable pieces of information you can have. This means that on your website you need to have a place for people to sign up.

Because people receive so much spam email, we have found that simple is better. The more professional or pretty emails do not work as well. A great option is to hire a copywriter off Upwork and have them write three to five campaign templates that you can use to convert leads into inventory.

Email campaigns are a great way to keep in touch with prospects and continue collecting useful marketing data during the low season. The insights you gain from this data can steer your marketing strategy for the high season.

Here are the six key elements of email marketing.

Step 1: Grow Your Email List

If you purchase an email list from a list broker, make sure you follow the email guidelines put forward in the Can-

Spam act and allow people to opt out if they choose. Even though I have never seen this be an issue, use an email address that is not connected with your domain just in the odd chance it could get blacklisted.

However you choose to do it, building your email list is critical. There are some great platforms out there that will help you with this. These include: Hubspot, Mailchimp, Constant Contact, Lemlist, SendinBlue, and Mailshake.

Step 2: Segment Your Lists

Create lists that target the right people. We touched on this earlier but some practical ways you can do this include segmenting by property. Lump all your condo owners in one group, and golf course community people in another.

List segmentation will increase your open and click rates, and decrease your unsubscribes.

Step 3: Make Your Subject Line Stand Out

When it comes to email open and click rates, your subject lines are everything. Your job is to make your subject lines stand out.

- Here are some tips for crafting creative subject lines:
- Entice curiosity, but don't be too clever. You want to make them curious enough to open and click, but without being so cryptic that the subscriber hasn't a clue as to what you're talking about.
- Include numbers. There is something about numbers that draw the eye.
- Use a friendly and conversational tone.

- Speak in the language and style that your subscribers use themselves, especially when talking with their friends.

Step 4: Have a Message Worth Reading

Keep in mind that as they open your email, you are just one of fifty they received that day. This is why your messaging should be personal.

Inject some personality to engage them. With email, I have found that less is more. Avoid making a beautiful email template that looks great on the screen but blends in with every other advertisement they see.

Instead, include some of the tips covered in the direct mail marketing section and offer a unique call to action.

Step 5: Be Personal

No one likes to receive an email that says, "Dear Sir" or "Dear Madam." It is too general. Instead, be different and personalize people's names, area, community, and building.

When you draft your subject line and message content, it's natural to think of the thousands of people who are about to receive it. However, it's far more effective to write as if speaking to an individual person, with a personal subject line and a personalized message.

To write this way, you'll have to really know your buyer persona. You need to understand their problems, their desires, their values, their likes, and their dislikes.

If you have trouble with this, send out an email asking for a quick five-minute chat. On the call, you can ask questions that will help you understand what your subscribers' needs are, and how they think.

Spending a day or two talking with your subscribers will be time well spent because it will help you so much – not only with your messaging but also with creating or improving your products and services.

Step 6: Optimize for Mobile

Mobile email accounts for 67% of all email opens, depending on your target audience, product, and email type. You simply can't afford to ignore your mobile users. You must appeal to them.

Make sure your email is responsive and includes easily loadable media. Also consider the fact that mobile screens are smaller, so long subject lines may get cut off on mobile devices.

Here are some more tips for appealing to mobile users:

- Keep the formatting simple (single-column), under 600 pixels wide.

- Use a larger font. Small fonts are difficult to read on mobile.

- Don't assume images are being displayed (Android turns images off by default). Make sure it looks good without them.

- Use smaller images to reduce load time.

- Use a large call-to-action button. Larger buttons are easier to tap with a thumb.

- Don't place two links next to, or on top of one another. That way, the user won't tap the wrong one by accident.

All these tips can help any campaign get better open rates, but don't get discouraged if you don't see a turnaround right away.

Email marketing is an art and science, so give yourself some wiggle room to experiment and find what tactics work best for your business and your subscribers.

PAY PER CLICK MARKETING

Next on the list is pay-per-click marketing or PPC. This is an important part of your inventory growth strategy.

PPC works because people have high intent when they are searching for something. People are looking to solve their problem and they want to find a property manager the moment they perform that search. If someone Googles "vacation rental management companies in my area" that person is obviously a much higher quality lead than the individual looking for coffee shops. The reason that paid search traffic works so well is that people are actively searching for exactly what you have to offer. Many marketing sources are "Interruption marketing" where you're aiming to pull their attention away from something (TV show, Facebook scrolling, etc.) to something else. Paid search ads are one of the only advertising channels that are the answer which the person is seeking. The problem is there are only so many people who are looking to list their home as a vacation rental (or with a property manager) and so the search volume is low.

The most common form of PPC is Google Ads. If you are new to PPC, this is where I would suggest you start. Create an account and build out the campaigns that will be most effective. The goal is to cast as wide a net as possible, and use a service like Ahrefs or Semrush to know those right keyword terms.

At Vintory, we've found there's a handful of keywords in each market that earn the majority of the searches of homeowners looking for a new vacation rental manager. But, the long tail of demand often leads us to finding anywhere from 50-70 unique keywords in each market to earn some searches every quarter. Due to the fact that the search volume and audience size that you're targeting is so small, make sure to set up the right keywords in your campaign to cover all of the relevant keywords homeowners are looking for. We've found searches around Airbnb management, co-hosting and STR or short term rentals are more common today than even a year or two ago, leading to better performance in paid search.

While many view PPC as a gamble and approach it with a "pay and pray" approach, the truth is that PPC is very effective when run properly. PPC is simply targeting the right owner at just the right time as they are searching for a solution. As a result, based on our data, PPC traffic has some of the highest conversion rates of any digital ad traffic source.

LIST-BASED RETARGETING

List-based retargeting is more specific than retargeting, and it has been a game changer for all our Vintory partners. Previously, the only way to get in front of your prospect targets was through direct mail.

Now, with list-based retargeting, you can utilize Facebook, Instagram, Twitter, and LinkedIn to serve up display ads directly to your target audience by uploading a list of your target prospects and customers. There are different places you might run these ads. Facebook and Instagram use a feature called Custom Audiences, Twitter uses Tailored Audiences, and Linkedin uses Matched Audiences.

My recommendation is to use Google Tag Manager to centralize installing and deploying these tracking tags and pixels to your website and landing pages. This makes everything less complicated and lets you see everything in one place without having to hire a developer.

This step is all about honing in on your data. You are casting a specific net for people who are interested in what you have to offer. It's making sure you are restricting the ad platforms to only target your audience.

Even if they have never visited your site, if you have a contact's name, email, and phone number, you can serve display ads directly to them.

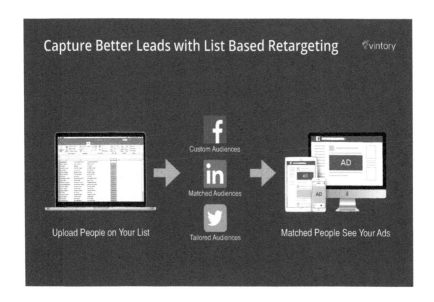

1. Content is king. The number of leads you convert will be directly related to your messaging. Remember, this is cold traffic that hasn't heard of your company or brand before. So they're not likely to convert after seeing a single message or ad.

2. Deliver hyper-focused messaging and content. Move away from using ads to showcase your company as a whole. Pick a single service or offering and demonstrate how that will provide value to your potential customers.

3. Use Lead-gen ads. These types of ads are lead magnets that will offer your potential customers something like an e-book in exchange for their contact information. Remember, this approach is all about delivering value and deepening your relationship with your customers.

IP TARGETING

This brings us to IP Targeting. I often joke that if the CIA were ever to get into the marketing business, this is the place they would start! Just the title sounds invasive and even a tad creepy.

Many people have not even heard of this. IP targeting allows you to serve up display ads directly on your prospective owner's computers as they surf the web. This means you can have a customer looking at ESPN and still see your ad.

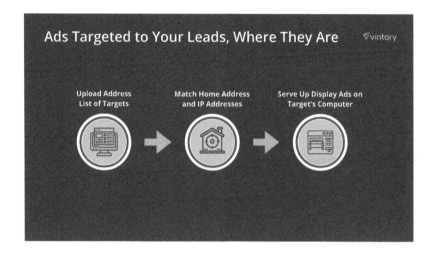

All you have to do is upload a list of your targets to the IP targeting software. This software then matches your target with an IP address. From there, the software serves display ads to the targeted devices using the IP address. It's unbelievable! If you do not know where to start, Simplifi and AdCellerant are two companies that offer IP targeting.

This is a big deal. It means someone does not have to visit your website and get "cookied" to receive your information. Aside from large venture capital companies and Vintory clients, very few companies in the vacation rental industry are doing this!

RETARGETING

Because 80-95% of the leads who visit your landing page will not fill out your form, retargeting is critical.

Retargeting is a cookie-based technology that uses

simple code on your website that allows you to advertise to people who have visited your website in the past. Simply insert the code into your website and every time a visitor comes to your desired landing page, they will receive a browser cookie. This cookie will tell your retargeting advertising provider when to re-market to your website visitors as they continue to visit other sites. These advertisements might appear as display ads or banner ads depending on what you've chosen, and there are many types of retargeting advertising options out there. The goal of these advertisements is to bring your potential customers back to your website for them to learn more about your services.

Retargeting is very effective at brand-building and awareness and the costs are relatively inexpensive per click and per impression. The deeper you go, the more focused you can target homeowners. You can focus on those homeowners who have visited your site in just the past few weeks and better utilize your resources.

However, this only works if your landing page actually generates traffic. If no one shows up to view your site, it does not matter how effective your retargeting strategy might be. Keep this in mind because platforms like Google, Facebook, AdRoll, and others require a certain level of traffic to protect the anonymity of website visitors.

CONCLUSION

I know this chapter was a bit heavy. But my goal is to demonstrate how you can level the playing field against your competition. All the big companies you compete against do this.

It's no secret I would suggest Vintory as a great option to take care of all your marketing needs. But even if you go a different direction, do something! Get away from the "pay and pray" approach and be strategic in how you market to others. Bring cohesion to your marketing process by making sure your direct mail, email, PPC, list-based retargeting, and IP targeting work in tandem with one another.

13

INBOUND
MARKETING

CHAPTER THIRTEEN

Inbound Marketing

"WHAT WE WANT YOU TO DO IS TO CHANGE THE MODE OF YOUR WEBSITE FROM A ONE-WAY SALES MESSAGE TO A COLLABORATIVE, LIVING, BREATHING HUB."

— Brian Halligan with Hubspot

As great as omnichannel outbound marketing can be, there is another form of marketing that is very effective – inbound marketing. According to a study of over nine-hundred marketing professionals, Hubspot discovered inbound marketing costs average 61% less per lead than traditional outbound marketing.[32]

Inbound marketing is a great long-term strategy that, unfortunately, few VRMs will ever do. It is hard, it takes time, but it works.

---

32   https://blog.hubspot.com/blog/tabid/6307/bid/31555/
Inbound-Leads-Cost-61-Less-Than-Outbound-New-Data.aspx

So, what is inbound marketing? According to Hubspot, "Inbound marketing is a business methodology that attracts customers by creating valuable content and experiences tailored to them. While outbound marketing interrupts your audience with content they don't always want, inbound marketing forms connections they are looking for and solves problems they already have."[33] Inbound marketing is attracting customers with valuable content and experiences that are tailored to meet their needs. It is solving a problem they have, and delivering the right information at the right time of the buyer's journey.

Over the past decade, as the power has shifted from the seller to the buyer, the switch from outbound to inbound marketing has only accelerated. This is the way people want to buy. They prefer a research-based strategy as opposed to a seller contacting them and using pressure tactics to get them to sign up for a service they might not need. In the words of Brian Halligan, CEO and co-founder of Hubspot, "The bottom line is that people are sick and tired of being interrupted with traditional outbound marketing messages and have become quite adept at blocking marketers out!"[34]

Again, omnichannel outbound marketing is still effective and necessary in the vacation rental industry, but inbound marketing should be part of your long-term marketing strategy.

---

33   https://www.hubspot.com/inbound-marketing
34   Brian Halligan, Inbound Marketing: Get Found Using Google, Social Media, and Blogs. (p.6)

THE BASICS OF INBOUND MARKETING

Because Hubspot has written the manual for inbound marketing, I lean on their philosophy for my own approach. They state: "The inbound methodology can be applied in three ways:

1. **Attract:** drawing in the right people with valuable content and conversations that establish you as a trusted advisor with whom they want to engage

2. **Engage:** presenting insights and solutions that align with their pain points and goals so they are more likely to buy from you

3. **Delight:** providing help and support to empower your customers to find success with their purchase"[35]

These three steps form the foundation for the way Vintory approaches inbound marketing. Our goal is to craft material and package it in such a way that people want to view what we have. Unlike clickbait advertisements that lure a potential customer in, but deliver little payoff, our goal at Vintory is to provide material that exceeds expectations.

If the concept of inbound marketing is new to you, start small. Think about your buyer and their unique pain points. What are those questions you keep hearing? Then make a plan to attract, engage, and delight your audience.

---

35   https://www.hubspot.com/inbound-marketing

START WITH INTERACTIVE CONTENT

The best bang for your buck in inbound marketing comes down to interactive content. This is by far the quickest and easiest way to implement an inbound marketing strategy. Building trust and establishing expertise is one of the most important ways to develop a relationship with a high-quality lead. It's adding value right away.

Several examples come to mind. The first is my friend David Angotti with SmokyMountains.com. David did something unique and created a fall foliage prediction map that gives viewers an estimate of when leaves will change colors in all areas of the United States. It is fantastic! While it took a lot of work to put together, it has seen tremendous payoff. To date, this map has received millions of visitors. The result is that companies keep coming back to this map and it drives a tremendous amount of traffic to his site.

Sometimes, the content marketing idea is right under a VRM's nose. I think of my friend CJ Stam with Southern Comfort Cabin Rentals. As Vintory worked with his team, his business development representative expressed frustration over a particular problem she faced. Every week she was inundated with questions from people asking how certain properties they were interested in buying were performing.

This was a nuisance to her because she would go to all the work of creating an individual Pro Forma, send it off to the person who requested it, and seldom hear anything back. Seeing this as an opportunity, our Vintory team created an interactive map using a simple drag and drop software called BatchGeo. This map contained the top twenty properties on the real estate market in CJ's area and we attached rental projections to each of these properties.

Moving forward, every person who called CJ's business development representative for information about properties currently on the market, could then be referred to their webpage to see an estimate. What we found was that most of the people contacting CJ were real estate agents. By having a means to retarget them, and collect their emails, we gleaned invaluable information, and flipped an annoyance into a win.

Vintory's COO, Randy Bonds, created an interactive calculator for his previous vacation rental management company. The way he had it set up, a potential owner could go to the website, enter some parameters such as the nightly rate, occupancy, and commission, and it would tell you what the property would earn or cost you per month.

These are just a few of many examples I could list of interactive content.

A FIVE-STEP GUIDE TO CONTENT MARKETING

Let's be real. We all swim through oceans of content every day as we scroll through the internet and social media. With a sharp eye we can always tell what content was strategically designed for an audience and what content was fired wishfully into the ether.

While accessibility levels the playing field, those with a content strategy are playing a different game than those who have none.

Whether you have a content strategy in place, or you've just started one, it's important to always revisit your plan to make sure it's innovative and hitting the mark. Instead of just adding to the sea of content that's out there – use your content strategy to improve brand awareness, increase conversions, and boost your revenue.

Here are several steps you should take:

Step 1: Create Homeowner Personas

Aside from those days in my youth when I may or may not have delivered the occasional prank call, I have never picked up the phone, dialed a number at random, and delivered a message to whoever answers. It almost seems ridiculous to say this. Yet, it is essentially what many marketers do every day.

If this has been your strategy, it's time to change. Start

by breaking down the intended recipient of your message by demographic, geographic, psychographic (lifestyle), and behavioral segments. For each of our partners at Vintory, we build out homeowner personas. It is worthwhile to learn if your market is full of what we call "First Time Franks" or do-it-yourselfers like "RBO Ruby." This information changes what, how, and where you deliver what you want to say.

Every data point you learn about your target market sharpens your message. It is your job to learn where they hang out both socially and digitally, and what messages resonate with them. Is your audience looking for expertise? Are they younger and thus gravitate toward visual content?

Regardless, the inbound marketing content you create should be visually appealing, quickly scannable, and interesting for it to be click-worthy to your key target market.

Step 2: Decide Your Aims

Your strategy must have a guiding aim. Ask yourself: What do I want to achieve? Full occupancy rentals, followers, increased inventory, exposure, brand awareness, or market dominance? What is your overarching aim? At Vintory, prior to discussing content or tactics, we begin each partner relationship by establishing a list of goals. Set your sights on crafting a message that is relatable to your audience.

Step 3: Deliver Your Message

Humanizing content is the challenge. With every property management company across the U.S. pumping out content, it can be difficult to stand apart from the pack. Ultimately, you need to open a dialogue with your clients and build a relationship.

Great content isn't a one-way street; it goes both ways. It involves doing the little things well, such as: Asking questions, responding to emails or direct messages in a timely manner, and responding to every interaction as a person and not just as a company. Remember that guests and homeowners want to like and trust you before they do business with you.

People respond to being impressed, heard, helped, inspired, and entertained. Do all you can to create interest and intrigue into your brand with a relatable or emotion eliciting message. Tease out promotions, and develop funnels to attract to your website or get in touch.

Step 4: Keep It Simple and Learn Fast

Overcomplicating and overcommitting are just going to stifle your progress. This may even cause people to turn you off altogether. Make sure your plan is realistic, within your schedule, and for your team.

If it is your first time carrying out a content strategy, I would encourage you to review your progress after three months. Conduct a social or content audit. What worked? Who did my Facebook ads reach? Who read my blogs? What times were successful posts shared and on what days of the week? Scrutinize and optimize the plan, because the next three months should be more effective. Consider building a content calendar from here on out.

Step 5: Create a Content Calendar

Content calendars are living documents that map out all the marketing activities for your organization. Its purpose is not only to ensure tactics are organized and executed, but also to manage which messages are going out into the marketplace and when.

Content calendars help to ensure you are delivering a consistent online voice that will enhance your brand, while also anticipating seasonal trends that will maximize content effectiveness. They improve the quality of your content, because planning in advance usually means fewer errors and more creative ideas. Not to mention that this is a resource to coordinate all members of your team – sales, marketing, leadership – to provide oversight for your messaging and to visualize how your content and channels will work together.

When it comes to the technology used to create a content calendar, there are a lot of options out there. From Google Calendars to customized spreadsheets, whichever platform you choose, it's crucial to not only map out upcoming dates and deliverables, but to record your results.

Here are some ideas:

- Start with recurring tactics such as blog posts, newsletters, or email blasts.

- Identify the frequency and timing of message delivery.

- Plan out any significant or unique campaigns such as during the holiday season.

- Map out which channels will be publishing content and when.

- Look for gaps in your calendar, or times where too much is going on.

IF YOU NEED HELP, ASK

Knowing what content to write, post, share, or even gather can be a headache for many vacation rental property managers. While managing vacation rentals is your wheelhouse and where you nail it every time, converting and managing successful content might not be.

One of the biggest knocks on business owners and managers is waiting too long to ask for help. That doesn't need to be the case for you. There are so many platforms out there that can lend you a hand for an affordable rate.

If the entire concept of inbound marketing seems like it is beyond your limitations, reach out to one of the team members at Vintory, and we can get you started in the right direction.

14

REFERRAL
MARKETING

CHAPTER FOURTEEN

Referral Marketing

"PEOPLE INFLUENCE PEOPLE. NOTHING INFLUENCES PEOPLE MORE THAN A RECOMMENDATION FROM A TRUSTED FRIEND. A TRUSTED REFERRAL INFLUENCES PEOPLE MORE THAN THE BEST BROADCAST MESSAGE. A TRUSTED REFERRAL IS THE HOLY GRAIL OF ADVERTISING."

– Mark Zuckerberg

This extended conversation on marketing takes us to the highest quality of leads a VRM can generate – personal referrals.

Referral marketing is a form of marketing that uses your network to spread the word about your business. Rather than relying on traditional forms of advertising, you include the people you know, such as customers, realtors, and influencers, to generate leads.

Nothing can quite compete with a word-of-mouth old school referral. This is why building those relationships with realtors in your market will do much to determine your success. When a realtor (or someone else others trust) says you are the go-to person for vacation home rentals, that is the greatest lead you can generate.

It is estimated that word-of-mouth referrals make up 20-50% of most purchasing decisions. Needless to say, referrals from realtors are a huge source of deals and should not be overlooked.

KEYS TO BUILDING GREAT RELATIONSHIPS WITH REALTORS

One key relationship with a realtor can turn into a cash cow, generating dozens of leads per year. So, create a proactive realtor referral program. How do you do this? Here are a few steps.

First, add them to your regular owner outreach! Make sure realtors are on your direct mail list and receive the same postcards you send to property owners. This increases the chance they will pass your card along to their clients. Make sure your name is top of mind when talk of renting out a home ever comes up.

Second, create specific campaigns just for them. We have already talked about the importance of having a great email database. Do this with your realtors. Add them to all of your omnichannel marketing campaigns.

Third, offer them incentives and referral fees. I mentioned earlier that some VRMs fear handing our referral fees because they feel it might be a waste of cash. Trust me, the math pencils out, and the ROI is there. The key is to know your CAC and what the projection will be for this new piece of inventory. Suddenly, handing out $500 does not look so bad.

Fourth, never forget the rule of reciprocity. According to Robert Cialdini, the rule of reciprocity says, "We should try to repay, in kind, what another person has provided us." [32] If you give agents referrals first, they will feel obligated to return that favor.

One of my favorite sayings is "give before you get."

Fifth, give them tools they need to be successful. This goes hand in hand with my previous point. Ask yourself: What is a pain point for a realtor I can help solve? Find solutions for your realtors and I guarantee you will receive leads in return.

ASK THE BIG QUESTION

On a scale from one to ten, how likely are you to recommend us to a friend? That question is the meat and bones of one of the most important benchmarks of most companies – how customers feel about the overall sentiment of your brand.

You are probably familiar with the Net Promoter Score (NPS) and how companies use it to measure and improve

---

32   Robert Cialdini, *Influence: The Psychology of Persuasion.* *P.17.*

customer loyalty. NPS measures how many people who interact with your business, including your own employees, would tell their friends about your company and bring in new customers.

This matters because 83% of people who responded to Nielsen's Global Trust in Advertising Report stated they trust recommendations from family and friends more than any other kind of advertising.[33] This begs the question: how much are you investing in generating referrals?

DON'T JUST EXPECT REFERRALS TO HAPPEN

Referrals don't just happen. You might get the odd one or two from out of nowhere, but in almost every instance, quality referrals come from people with whom you have developed a relationship.

Too many businesses expect that if they offer great service, the referrals will come. If this were true, growing any business would be easy! My experience tells me that's not the case, and as with any business goal or strategy, a plan is necessary in order to reach your revenue goals.

So how do you get your referral flywheel started? There are three steps I recommend:

Step 1: Always Keep a Referral Mindset

You never know where your next lead might come from. It's important to look at every interaction as an opportunity for a potential referral or new lead. Companies that have

33   https://www.nielsen.com/ca/en/

referral programs report that up to 40% of their income comes from this one source. Build your network with everyone you encounter. Whether it's owners, guests, or people you meet in your everyday life.

While it's important to target the right leads, it's equally as important to check any preconceived notions about who will be able to make referrals. Always keep this referral mindset and instill this in your own team. I recently chatted with one company who built out an incredible referral program through their housekeeping team.

Don't miss an opportunity to help anyone who is part of, or interacts with, your company make a referral.

Step 2: Build a Referral Process

A referral process is not only necessary to incentivize and reward those who bring in referrals, but also to track and nurture these leads. When you create your referral process, do the following things:

First, create a guide that explains the referral process for employees, and how they can direct their referrals. This should include information, such as: possible referral sources, tips for speaking about your services and brand, and what incentives to offer.

Second, capture the referral. Keeping referrals organized is key to converting them into leads. Referrals come from many different places, but you will need to log them all in one system. One of the best ways to do this is to automate your referral process digitally by setting up a form on your website for your referral program, and linking this form directly to your CRM.

Third, nurture those leads. Getting a referral in the door

is only half the work. You need to put a process in place to nurture this new lead. How will your team reach out? How often will they try to contact the lead? How long will you keep them on your system? Automated touchpoints through a CRM are one of the best ways to ensure that no lead falls through the cracks.

Fourth, offer referral rewards. It's important to determine what incentive program you will have in place for your team and your customers to make referrals. For example, when a customer refers a friend to Airbnb, they get a $20 credit. Not all referrals are equal and not all referrals will become customers, so it's important to determine what benchmarks you have for offering a reward.

Step 3: Use Analytics to Refine Your Strategy

Your referral process should not end once you close your lead. Over time you should pay close attention to what referral sources bring in the greatest revenue and what relationships prove to be the most valuable.

Once you identify the sources that bring in the most referrals, you can invest more time and money into nurturing these relationships.

A GREAT REFERRAL PROGRAM EXAMPLE

Some companies do a great job of this, and I notice. One of the best examples of a referral program I've seen is from my friend Steve Schwab with Casago. Steve built out a program called "*Lifetime of Leads.*" Here's how it works. First, reach out to several of the top realtors in your market. Offer to take them to lunch or coffee, and explain that you are going to help them close more deals. For every property they refer to you, that property becomes their "lead machine." They will be seen by dozens if not hundreds of guests per year for every property they refer. Every guest that books that property, will see their information and you'll help them highlight their services. If they refer two properties, it only compounds from there. After several referrals, this becomes one of their top performing referral sources of leads.

Their contact information is seen in four different ways:

- At Booking – When a client receives an email confirming their reservation, the agent's contact information will be included in the email.

- At Check-in – When the guest receives check-in information and door code information, they will also be provided with the agent's contact information.

- In the Home – A tent card will be placed strategically in the home with the agent's information as well as a QR Code to see the top performing vacation homes currently on the market.

- At Check-Out – After check-out, guests will receive a survey, along with when they would like information about purchasing real estate in the local area. If they indicate interest, your agent information will be sent to them.

15

WHAT TO DO WHEN
PEOPLE CALL

CHAPTER FIFTEEN

What to Do When People Call

"PEOPLE BUY FROM PEOPLE THEY TRUST. PEOPLE TRUST THOSE THEY LIKE AND PEOPLE LIKE THOSE THEY CONNECT WITH."

– Jeff Bloomfield

O ur business development leader, Jade Wolff, is a model for best sales practices. A while back, she went through the process of secretly shopping one hundred vacation rental management companies and inquired about their property management services. The results were shocking. Only about 34% of VRMs picked up the phone. When she left a message, only 57% of the VRMs called her back. 50% of the time she never made a connection.

Here was the real kicker. When Jade called the

big venture-backed conglomerates like Vacasa, she experienced a 100% connectivity rate. This did not surprise me in the least. Big vacation rental companies are big for a reason. They know the value of inventory. It's not that they offer a much better service than your average VRM. They just take the time to answer the phone.

Back in 2011, Harvard Business Review "audited 2,241 U.S. companies, measuring how long each took to respond to a web-generated test lead. Although 37% responded to their lead within an hour, and 16% responded within one to 24 hours, 24% took more than 24 hours – and 23% of the companies never responded at all. The average response time, among companies that responded within 30 days, was 42 hours."[32]

Considering the average cost for a lead in our industry is $200-$300 or more and the opportunity cost of losing a piece of inventory can be tens of thousands of dollars, it amazes me that more vacation rental companies do not have a better system in place to capture their leads.

Think of a pro baseball athlete who steps to the plate to take a swing. There is a reason they use a full bat. If they were to cut their bat in half, they would have a much lesser chance of making contact. It's the same in sales. If you only respond half of the time to people who inquire, your odds of hitting a home run are greatly reduced.

Here is why responding to leads is so important. Mark Roberge, author of *The Sales Acceleration Formula*, a Harvard Professor on Sales, and Former Chief Revenue Officer at Hubspot, said the following: "There have been numerous studies done about sales and leads. One by MIT and another one by InsideSales.com and they all pretty

---

32   https://hbr.org/2011/03/the-short-life-of-online-sales-leads

much say the same thing. If you call a lead back within two minutes, the likelihood of success is like ten times more than if you wait an hour. And about 10,000 times more likely if you wait a day."[33]

If you cannot afford to have someone answer the phones full time, I recommend hiring a company like Extenteam to help ensure you are answering every call 24 hours a day.

This will make sure no lead slips through the cracks simply because you failed to answer the phone.

MAKE SURE YOUR PROCESS IS CLEAR

Assuming you are one of those VRMs who does answer the phone, the next question you might have is, "What do I do now?"

Some VRMs utilize a phone tree system that makes homeowners go through a series of prompts to speak with someone. For example, if a property owner hears prompts for the sales department and rental department, they might not be sure which one to pick and you increase the risk they might hang up in frustration.

Ultimately, poor phone tree systems end up giving leads a poor first impression and they might hang up after making a snap judgment that this company is a mess.

If you utilize a phone tree for your business, you should listen to your system every so often and place yourself in

33   Mark Roberge on Churn.FM podcast - https://www.churn.fm/episode/how-to-drive-revenue-growth-through-customer-retention

the shoes of a property owner that knows nothing about the business. Make an option on the main menu that says, "Press 3 to learn more about our vacation rental management services."

If the call is not picked up by the business development representative, it should ring in the reservations department. Unfortunately, very few VRMs train their reservations staff to capture owner leads. What generally happens is the reservationists take down the property owners contact info so that someone can call them back later. But as soon as this happens, the chances of converting this new lead plummet. This lead is on a mission for information, and it is unlikely you will convert them through a game of phone tag. They want their questions answered, and they want them answered now.

I recommend creating a shared sheet or other resources that has a snippet of info on each aspect of every service you offer. This way a reservationist can do the basics and at least read off this info to people who call. They do not have to provide all the information, but they should provide enough so that the homeowner is satisfied and has a reason to talk to the business development representative.

If you are the owner or manager of a company that manages vacation rentals, keep these insights in mind and use them to be more competitive.

THE TOP 10 SALES TIPS

Let's assume you are the VRM or business development rep and you have an owner who is on the line. How do you respond? What should you tell them? What should you avoid?

Going back to my business development rep, Jade, here are ten tips she recommends. These will help you close your deals at a higher rate and get you started off on the right note with your new homeowner.

Tip 1: Make a Great First Impression

We all make snap judgements. It's part of human nature. But things go a lot smoother if you inspire confidence from the beginning. This starts by answering the phone. Research shows that about 75% of people do not leave messages. First-hand experience has taught me that most owners believe if you do not answer the phone on their first call that you are unlikely to be there for them when they need you the most.

Tip 2: Be Professional

Answer the phone with a professional greeting that states the company's name. Don't just say, "Hello" or "Bob here." Remember that it's all about first impressions. If they view you as professional from the start, they can look forward to that professionalism throughout the duration of their contract agreement.

Tip 3: Stay in Control

Another reason it's important to use the company's name in the greeting is because the homeowner may wonder if they have called the right place. If the caller has to ask if they are calling the right place, they are the one asking questions and gain control of the conversation. The best salespeople understand that staying in control and leading the conversation is key to a swift and successful sales process. Ask questions and be a good listener, seek to understand and not simply to respond. Control is not pushy, it's confidence and leadership, and it's helpful.

Tip 4: Use an Appropriate Tone of Voice

One of the best tools a persuader has is the way they use their voice. Remember that it's all about communication and most of the time we are selling over the phone, and don't have body language to rely on. Tone is not just to influence, it's also for making others feel at ease. We want to slow our cadence for people that have a slow cadence like the elderly because that's the frequency they hear. Anything faster than how they talk will not compute. And we need to speed it up for people that are talking fast, otherwise they may get impatient or lose interest. Sometimes we need to up our tone to be bubbly, inquisitive and engaging. Other times, we should use a low tone when we mean business, and when we want to be firm on contract negotiations.

Tip 5: Use Mirroring and Labeling Techniques

Mirroring is when we repeat the last three words of what someone says in an inquisitive way. People feel we are paying attention, and asking questions keeps us in control. Labeling is when we listen and make a statement to acknowledge what they said. Use these key phrases: "It looks like," "It seems like," and "It feels like." Try observational language, such as: "It seems like you care more about the care of the home than the money it could make." If you can get someone to say, "That's right," you've got them.

Tip 6: Know Your Stuff

Product knowledge gives you confidence to talk to any lead, and have genuine enthusiasm for the product or service. Pointing out your favorite product features and comparing them to other inferior products or services shows you know your stuff and inspires confidence in your buyer. This will also put a homeowner at ease so that they will not want to waste their time shopping around.

Tip 7: Offer Two Yeses

One of the best ways to secure a commitment is through using what I call the "two yeses." Give someone two options that are both what you want, and they are more likely to choose one. Avoid yes or no questions that leave room for nos. This works especially well for setting appointments. Saying, "Do you prefer to meet on a Friday or Saturday?" is much better than saying, "Can we meet and what day is best for you?" Keep offering two or more options that narrow the time or commitment until you have what you want.

Tip 8: Challenge Them

Yes, it's important to be a good relationship builder, but experts say it's far more important to be willing to challenge someone's ideas in favor of your own. As long as you use your tone in a friendly way, you won't turn someone off when you give them a little push. If you don't challenge them a little, you are likely to have them take no action or lose them all together. Plus, the real selling doesn't start until someone says no and we've got to be ready for that with some counter ideas to win them over.

Tip 9: Be Persistent with Follow-up

Only 10% of success comes from a great first impression

and conversation. The other 90% comes from diligent follow up and follow through. Statistically you need to call someone eight times to get back in touch with them and 40% of leads are only called twice. It's easy to get sidetracked with hotter leads as they come in but reaching back to do follow ups instead of always charging forward will win you more deals.

Tip 10: No Means No... Except for Sales

To me, no doesn't mean no in sales. It means not right now. I make a follow up task to check back with them after the summer or every six months. Things change for people and if you are staying in touch, you'll be the convenient one to talk to and can assist them when they are ready. Design a long-term nurturing drip email that has value for them. Pass on articles from online resources that are relevant to them. Staying in touch is a great way to ask for referrals as well. Just because they aren't ready, doesn't mean they don't know someone who is.

WHEN YOU FACE OBJECTIONS

Granted, some people will push back. When they do, here are a couple of strategies you can implement.

Strategy #1 - The Ask

Find out exactly why someone has an objection. If you phrase your question skillfully, and use a pleasant tone, you'll be surprised to learn what's really at the core of their objection.

Strategy #2 - Build Value

When someone is stuck on price, the antidote is to build value. Price is irrelevant if the service can make more money for the client.

Strategy #3 - Imagine

Paint a picture of how wonderful things could be with us as their partner. Use the word "imagine" as you describe how good it could be. "Imagine your home as the backdrop of a family's quality time together." "Imagine your property magically taking care of itself and paying its own bills." "Imagine your property waiting for you, clean, comfortable and full of money!"

Strategy #4 - Would You Rather

Like a game of choose the better option, lead your prospect through a thought exercise where you give them two choices. Always have them choose between a "yes" and a "yes" and lead them down the right path. This works especially well for setting appointments.

Strategy #5 - FOMO

Fear of missing out is real. Remind homeowners that their neighbors are doing well since they partnered with you. Point out that their place is even nicer, has a better location, and is more charming. Plant the seed that short term rental regulations are tightening all the time and if they are *grandfathered* in they will always have a seat at the table.

Rejections come in all different shapes and sizes. You might have people say, "Your fee is too high!" When this happens, ask some of the following questions: "What are you basing your opinion on?" "Are you a price shopper or a value shopper?" "Would you rather have a lower management fee and make less money? Or would you rather have a fee that was the average for the area and make a premium?"

A homeowner might say to you, "I can do it better myself." If this is the case, ask questions like, "Just out of curiosity, how can you be so sure?" "Is this property an investment or is it a hobby business?" "Imagine that you didn't have to do X. What would you do with all that extra free time and money?" "Wouldn't you rather have passive income instead of a second job?"

They might say, "I don't want to share my home with anyone." Respond with, "What exactly is it that you find uncomfortable?" Point out they can add value to your home by building rental data. "Can you imagine helping other families to make priceless memories while paying your property taxes with ease each year?" "Wouldn't you rather lock off some space for personal belongings and use the rest of the space to pay some bills and have your property paying for itself?" "Are you sure you want to miss out on the opportunity to do enough rentals to keep an active license and grandfather-in the property in case short term rental regulations tighten?"

WHY SALES MATTERS

At the end of the day, it all comes back to numbers. If you believe inventory is important, you will treat leads like they are gold. This is critical to your success.

Whenever I am on a sales call with a client, I try to do the basics well. I put a smile on my face before I pick up the phone. I try to ask the right questions that will give me the information I need to provide the maximum value.

Bottom line, I treat sales seriously because it is the heart and soul of our business. If we have no sales, we have no company. Even if you are great at selling to guests, maybe you undervalue property owners. If so, it's time to make a switch. Keep yourself grounded in the value of inventory.

Don't make people go through a list of prompts. Before the call, plan for success. Have your company's features and benefits list handy. Have a place to take notes. Check your tone, be pleasant. Put a mirror on your desk. Assume you will close the deal and that everything is okay. Paying attention to these simple practices will result in you closing more deals.

16

THE FUTURE IS
BRIGHT

CHAPTER SIXTEEN

The Future is Bright

"THE FUTURE IS THE FUTURE WE WILL."

– Peter Thiel

For years, vacation rental management was defined by seasoned talent. Established managers with years of experience were what owners wanted. However, as audiences and technologies change, millennials have brought much to the industry and will continue to bring innovations that attract new owners.

It is estimated millennials will make up 75% of the workforce by 2025. This should come as no surprise then that an increasing number of second homeowners and rental managers point out how the new generation is taking over the industry.

Millennials are a generation known for innovation and flexibility. Now, during a time of radical transformation, opportunity, and market competition, their skills are propelling the vacation rental industry into a new era.

Mom and pop investors turned VRMs are passing

on their property portfolio to their children. This is a generational shift we see across the industry. The older generation is ready to retire and is training up their children to continue the family business.

MILLENNIALS ENJOY STABILITY

Vacation rental management jobs provide the stability that many millennials crave. I have found that in addition to many taking over their family operations, there is another group of vacation rental managers that are starting their own businesses. They are partnering with real estate agents and connections in the industry to start opening doors to a new way of doing vacation rental business. The number of vacation rental management businesses in the US has consistently grown, and now sits at around 23,000.[32]

The "sharing economy" has changed the hospitality industry. Airbnb and other platforms have made it simple to find short term rentals and have opened new accommodation experiences that are more appealing to a new generation of travelers.

Worldwide, the sharing economy has seen over $12 billion in investment.[33] To put this in perspective, that is more than social networking startups such as Facebook and Twitter have received. This continued growth of investment shows the sharing economy is not going

32 https://www.hostfully.com/blog/state-u-s-vacation-rental-industry-2018/#:~:text=The%20total%20number%20of%20vacation,rental%20companies%20in%20the%20world.
33 https://www.hostfully.com/blog/state-u-s-vacation-rental-industry-2018/#:~:text=The%20total%20number%20of%20vacation,rental%20companies%20in%20the%20world.

anywhere.

Millennials understand this market. Younger generations coming out of University with staggering debts that average at $32,000 or much higher.[34] The idea of pursuing the "traditional life" and purchasing a home, seem unrealistic.

The younger generation has become enthralled with travel, they don't want to buy houses, they want to explore the world. One poll found that 78% of millennials would choose to spend money on a desirable event over a desirable purchase.[35]

Millennials know how to market their vacation rentals to this audience. Guests also feel comfortable interacting with VRMs who they feel understand their lifestyle needs. This makes millennials great at empathizing with guests and offering services and features in their rentals that will attract young guests.

MILLENNIALS ARE TECH SAVVY

Millennials are a generation that has witnessed significant changes in technology. They have grown with these new technologies and embraced them. And their ability to react to change and resourcefulness is a key factor in how they will succeed in the vacation rental management industry.

34   https://www.valuepenguin.com/average-student-loan-debt#:~:text=Average%20Student%20Loan%20Debt%20in%20The%20United%20States,outstanding%20in%20student%20loan%20debt.
35   https://www.cnbc.com/2017/09/07/millennials-would-rather-travel-than-buy-a-home.html#:~:text=Young%20people%20aren't%20buying,d%20rather%20travel%20the%20world&text=According%20to%20a%20recent%20survey,older%20who%20said%20the%20same.

In times of global change, millennials will be able to quickly implement new technologies to help travelers feel safe and at ease as they vacation.

Technology has become one of the greatest catalysts for growth in vacation rentals. Millennials understand what appeals to holidaymakers. Who better to lead the tech revolution in vacation rentals than the generation who grew up with constantly changing tech and seamlessly integrating it into their lives?

Some of the big trends in technology that millennials will help implement and make industry standards in the coming years include:

- **Payments** – Payment providers such as Stripe and MANGOPAY are used by just over half (51%) of managers. These tools make it simple for guests to book and pay for their short-term rental. It also adds a sense of security that their money is safe, using familiar payment gateways.

- **Keyless Entry** – 33% of managers now use keyless entry. This removes the clumsy key exchange that has been a struggle for the industry for many years. It provides a seamless check-in experience and removes some of the concerns for both managers and guests over in-person interactions when a global pandemic is present.

- **Dynamic Pricing Software** – Software that analyze rates and provide dynamic pricing will help with ensuring maximum profitability and occupancy rates for vacation rentals, keeping owners happy and increasing profits. Currently, 32% of managers use this software, but as millennials transition into decision making roles, we can expect this to become more prominent. Emerging technologies and new tools such as 3D tours, chatbots, and noise control devices will help improve customer service and provide heightened security.

- **AI and CRMs for Inventory Growth** – Most VRMs have pushed inventory growth to the side of their desk and are using post-it-notes, whiteboards, Google sheets, and postcards to track and attract new leads. Industry leading property acquisition platforms like **Vintory** are changing the inventory growth game, and it's AI and CRM technology like this that millennials easily adopt, while happily leaving whiteboards behind.

MILLENNIALS ARE FLEXIBLE AND INNOVATIVE

Not only did millennials grow up with tech, but they also came of age in an economic downturn. They have learned to do more with less. These problem-solving skills are paramount in the vacation rental industry and will help them succeed.

Relationship-management and fixing issues in a timely fashion as they arise are a large part of how managers spend their time. The problem-solving mentality of millennials lends itself well to dealing with owners and guests and swiftly reaching solutions.

WHY VINTORY MIGHT BE RIGHT FOR YOU

As the CEO of Vintory, it is my goal to revolutionize the vacation rental space and be a beacon of light for everyday vacation rental managers. Not just those who have been in the industry for decades, but those who are new to this space.

Vintory doesn't just offer software and services, we help build businesses, careers, and communities. Our vision is to accelerate the growth of the vacation rental market to become the preferred place to travel, work, play, dream, rest, and invest. We are well on our way to making our vision a reality through our mission to empower every professional vacation rental manager with the technology, expertise, and community they need to grow their inventory.

My story and the stories of many of our partners at Vintory show that growing your own vacation rental management business is hard, and managing the many demands that come with it is even harder. We built Vintory with this in mind.

My challenge to you is to stop your reservationist from playing digital marketing coordinator. Instead, get a master content strategist, brand storyteller, copywriter, graphic designer, data analyst, web developer, and more – all for what it would cost to hire a part-time assistant.

My team has made Vintory a simple-to-set-up, easy-to-use solution to cut the clutter and consistently add new properties to your program. It's the first and only CRM and Sales & Marketing Automation Platform designed exclusively for Vacation Rental Managers to grow their inventory. Grow smarter, faster, and bigger with built-in automation that will keep you organized and one step ahead of the competition. Capture more homeowners through our omnichannel marketing approach. Convert more leads with automatic lead nurturing and personalized AI. Know which campaigns are hitting the mark with centralized dashboards. Grow your business with half the effort.

Whether you're a new business, or growing enterprise, we support property management companies of all shapes and sizes. Our platform makes inventory growth easy, affordable, and tailored to your growth goals. Plus, we offer the support, training, and community you need. Supercharge your growth with our business network that is leveling the playing field for the independent professional property manager. It has never been easier to stay ahead of the competition, and to close more homeowner deals!

Inventory is everything. Without it, you will fail. But with it, there are no limits to your growth!

Appendix of Helpful Tools

It is important that you leverage the tools that are available to you. While Vintory offers most of these services on its platform, here are some tools I would recommend if you choose another option.

AdRoll is a marketing platform that makes retargeting simple and easy.

BatchGeo is a mapping tool that allows you to take information in a spreadsheet to a map in three simple steps. You can then embed this code into any website very easily.

Better Talent is a full-service hiring solution. They supercharge your hiring strategy by significantly increasing application flow while narrowing the applicant pool down to the perfect candidates. Their curated talent solution blends technology, behavioral science, and a high touch human element. They do the hard work of identifying and screening applicants so you can review vetted, ideal candidates to make the final call on who is the perfect fit.

Calconic is a simple calculator builder that you can embed into any website and use as a form of interactive content.

Calendly helps schedule appointments with qualified leads. There is a lot of friction with prospects on scheduling time. I always include calendars online so that people can book me. This cuts down on emails and puts the power in the hands of the lead.

CallRail is a form of call tracking. I recommend that with every postcard campaign you do, you create a separate phone number so that you can track the performance of each campaign. Another benefit is that it records every call you receive. So you can go back and listen if you missed anything.

Culture Index leverages psychometric personality assessments to use analytics instead of instincts to hire and manage teams.

Extenteam is an outsourcer for property management professionals operating short-term rentals. Their remote team members work exclusively for VRM's to supercharge their guest services, reservations, leasing, digital marketing, accounting, and other critical support functions.

Guest Ranger, Safely, Autohost use predictive analytics to prescreen guests before they even enter the door. They provide background checks, sex offender search, and ID verification. If this is meaningful to the owner, this gives you an advantage.

Lemlist is a tool used to send cold email outreach.

Loom is a video email. If you are having trouble getting hold of a prospect, you can highlight your entire rental program, show the pro formas in a video tailor to their needs. You might "provide hints of the best practices of a property listing" or "how to optimize a marketing channel."

Mailshake is similar to Lemlist and is a tool to allow you to send out cold email outreach.

NoiseAware alerts homeowners of loud or potentially harmful noises in their home. It is useful because it reduces the chances of parties and things getting out of hand.

The Predictive Index allows recruiters and companies to evaluate the personality traits and behavioral tendencies of a potential employee, to determine if they are the right fit.

Unbounce is a landing page builder. You can quickly and easily build landing pages and not know how to code.

Helpful Links

We have tons of resources and materials on the Vintory website. This collection of FREE resources will help all vacation rental managers in their quest to grow their inventory and add much needed revenue to their business – from Learning Studio Videos to past inventory growth webinars to downloadable templates. There are endless tools and strategies to target homeowners in your area and below you'll find just a sampling.

Vintory Learning Studio Resources

- https://vintory.com/resources/

Vintory YouTube Channel

- https://vintory.com/youtube

Vintory Blog

- https://vintory.com/our-blog/

ROI Calculator

- https://vintory.com/calculators/roi-estimator/

Valuation Calculator

- https://vintory.com/calculators/valuation-calculator/